**LEADING
WOMEN**

Founder of
Black Girls Code

*Kimberly
Bryant*

KATHRYN HULICK

Cavendish
Square

New York

Published in 2018 by Cavendish Square Publishing, LLC
243 5th Avenue, Suite 136, New York, NY 10016

Library of Congress Cataloging-in-Publication Data

Names: Hulick, Kathryn, author.
Title: Kimberly Bryant : founder of Black Girls Code / Kathryn Hulick.
Description: New York : Cavendish Square Publishing, [2018] | Series: Leading women | Includes bibliographical references and index.
Identifiers: LCCN 2017004028 (print) | LCCN 2017008747 (ebook) | ISBN 9781502627032 (library bound) | ISBN 9781502627049 (E-book)
Subjects: LCSH: Bryant, Kimberly, 1967---Juvenile literature. | Women engineers--United States--Biography--Juvenile literature. | African American engineers--United States--Biography--Juvenile literature. | Girls--Education--United States--Juvenile literature. | Minorities in science--United States--Juvenile literature. | Technical education--United States--Juvenile literature. | Black Girls Code (Organization)--Juvenile literature.
Classification: LCC TA140.B787 H85 2018 (print) | LCC TA140.B787 (ebook) | DDC 609.2 [B] --dc23
LC record available at https://lccn.loc.gov/2017004028

Editorial Director: David McNamara
Editor: Tracey Maciejewski
Copy Editor: Nathan Heidelberger
Associate Art Director: Amy Greenan
Designer: Lindsey Auten
Production Coordinator: Karol Szymczuk
Photo Research: J8 Media

The photographs in this book are used by permission and through the courtesy of: Cover, Fernanda Calfat/Getty Images; p. 1 courtesy, Kimberly Bryant; p. 4 Jeff Vespa/Getty Images; p. 8 Phil Stanziola, New York World-Telegram & Sun Collection, Library of Congress, Reproduction Number LC-USZ62-126558/File: Martin Luther King Jr. with medallion NYWTS.jpg/ Wikimedia Commons; p. 16 Vanderbilt/Collegiate Images/Getty Images; p. 28 Margaret Bartkowiak/Photoshot/Newscom; pp. 42, 48, 72 AP Photo/Bebeto Matthews; p. 53 Chip Somodevilla/Getty Images; p. 60 Angela Weiss/Getty Images; p. 64 Sonja Flemming/CBS/Getty Images; p. 69 Allison Shelley/Getty Images; p. 76 Monkey Business Images/Shutterstock.com; p. 80 Steve Jennings/Getty Images;p. 91 Noam Galai/WireImage/Getty Images.

Printed in the United States of America

CONTENTS

CHAPTER ONE

How a Revolution Begins

Kimberly Bryant is proud to be a nerd. She's an engineer who loves science fiction and going to the movies. To her, technology is more than just her career—it's cool. But unfortunately, she's an outlier. Just 3.5 percent of all working engineers and scientists in the United States are black women. Women of all races and ethnicities are less likely than men to work as scientists or engineers, but women of color—including African

Kimberly Bryant attends the annual *Glamour* Women of the Year event, which honors women who have made an impact on the world.

Americans, Hispanics, and American Indians—are almost completely missing from these important technical fields.

Bryant aims to change that. She founded the **nonprofit** Black Girls Code in 2011. The organization teaches coding, game design, robotics, and other tech skills to girls ages seven to seventeen from underrepresented communities. Since its founding, Black Girls Code has held numerous classes, workshops, and summer camps, and touched the lives of almost eight thousand girls. They've opened chapters in eleven cities in the United States as well as one in Johannesburg, South Africa. Some of the girls who have been through the program have launched their own apps online. Others are pursuing **computer science** degrees at competitive colleges and universities. "We believe teaching girls of color to code is revolutionary," Bryant says.[1] In fact, revolution is a theme that has colored her entire life, beginning with her childhood in Memphis, Tennessee.

The Struggle for Civil Rights

Kimberly Bryant grew up in the inner city of Memphis, raised by a single mother. She was born on January 14, 1967, just a day before the thirty-eighth birthday of Martin Luther King Jr., the inspiring and famous leader of the civil rights movement. This movement sought to provide equal rights for black Americans. In the 1950s, blacks living in the South had to follow laws that promoted segregation, oppression, and other forms of unfair and unequal treatment. For example, in Mississippi, white and black children had to attend separate schools. Poll taxes, literacy tests, and complicated registration systems prevented most black people from voting. These so-called Jim Crow laws also barred black people from certain housing, theaters, restaurants, stores, baseball fields, and even seats on the bus.

In December 1955, a woman named Rosa Parks had had enough of this unfair treatment. She was riding the bus home after a long day at work and refused to give up her seat so a white man could take it. This was against the law at the time. She was arrested, and her actions kicked off a bus boycott in Montgomery, Alabama, which ended with the city lifting the law. Buses were no longer segregated in Montgomery, but the fight for civil rights was just getting started. Martin Luther King Jr. had led the bus boycott. In January 1957, he became president of the Southern Christian Leadership Conference, a group of ministers and other activists who focused on nonviolent ways to promote equality. King quickly became a well-known and well-loved spokesperson for peaceful protest and civil rights.

In 1963, King organized the March on Washington for Jobs and Freedom. The march and rally ended with the famous speech "I Have a Dream," in which King said, "I have a dream that my four little children will one day live in a nation where they will not be judged by the color of their skin but by the content of their character."[2] In 1964, King was awarded the Nobel Peace Prize, and the United States Congress passed the Civil Rights Act,

This Medallion of Honor was one of the many awards Martin Luther King Jr. received for his contributions to the civil rights movement.

which made segregation in public places and employment **discrimination** illegal. However, fame made King a target for those who didn't agree with his ideas. On April 4, 1968, a little over a year after Kimberly Bryant was born, King was staying at the Lorraine Motel in Memphis. He stepped out onto the balcony, and was fatally shot.

Life in the Inner City

Though Bryant was too young to remember the incident, the fact that it occurred in her beloved hometown and the fact that King's birthday is so close to her own both seem like more than mere coincidences. "I like to think that revolutionary and radical action was running through my very veins, from the time I set foot on the Earth," she says.[3] Though the civil rights movement slowed after the 1960s, the feelings of excitement, anger, and pride that it had stirred up lingered in black communities. "My very upbringing was colored by this change of social upheaval and this radical shift in our common psyche both in my community and as a nation," says Bryant.[4] Even as a young person, she was a social activist. She got involved in student government and community organizations, and planned to be a lawyer.

At the time, she didn't realize engineering or computer science were options for her career. In the inner city where she lived, no one owned computers. She grew up in an area of the city called North Memphis, which Bryant says is a blighted area now. "There aren't too many kids that make it out," she says.[5] But, she and her siblings were different from their friends. They were smart and enjoyed school, so they were sent to special programs and took advanced placement classes. Her mother told them that excelling in school was the key to a good future. Bryant's older brother was the geek of the family, while she was the nerd. He was into video games, while she was into books and reading. Still, she would follow him around and go everywhere with him. She wanted to do what he did.

She was even jealous of his Christmas presents. "Every year as we opened the toys, I was always just enthralled by toys he received," Bryant says.[6] Examples included rock 'em sock 'em robots and chemistry sets. Bryant loved her own toys, too—in addition to being a nerd, she also played with dolls and kitchen sets as other young girls did. But she now realizes that she missed out on an opportunity to learn about science and technology from a young age. Though she was interested in these subjects, she was directed towards different activities deemed more appropriate for a girl growing up in the 1970s.

Bryant wound up following her brother into **electrical engineering** as a major, though it wasn't his example that led her to become an engineer. In fact, he eventually switched his major to communications. Bryant picked her major thanks to advice from her high school guidance counselors. Bryant excelled at math and science, so the counselors suggested that she look into engineering. They told her engineers would earn hefty salaries right out of college. So Bryant applied to the schools they suggested, and she earned a scholarship to attend Vanderbilt University.

The Women's Movement

The civil rights movement had afforded Bryant educational and career opportunities that she may not have had without those years of protest and activism. However, there was another barrier waiting to obstruct her path to success: she was a woman. At the same time that black people were fighting for equal rights during the 1960s, the women's movement, also known as the feminist movement, was challenging the traditional idea that a woman's duty was to care for her husband, children, and home. The women of this movement were fighting for equal rights for women in the workplace. In 1961, the dean of a medical school said, "We do keep women out, when we can. We don't want them here."[7] At the time, just 1 percent of engineers, 3 percent of lawyers, and 6 percent of doctors were women.

The women's movement gained momentum thanks to two important factors. First, a booming American economy during the 1970s and 1980s opened up many more jobs, and women were needed to fill them. In addition, access to reliable birth control in the form of oral contraceptives made it possible for women to complete their studies and establish careers before having children, or to choose not to have children at all. It began to be much more common for women to work in fields that once had been almost exclusively male, such as science and engineering.

The percentage of women working in most segments of science and engineering has climbed steadily over time. However, one field stands out as an exception to that rule: computer science. The percentage of women in the field has actually been falling since Kimberly Bryant graduated from Vanderbilt in the 1980s with her degree in electrical engineering and computer science. In 1984,

37 percent of bachelor's degrees in computer science went to women. By 2008, the number had fallen to just 18 percent. Most historians blame the drop on the fact that home computers, which started becoming popular in the 1980s, were marketed almost entirely to boys, not to girls. As a result, during the decades that followed, boys grew up playing with computers and learning about them, while girls were left behind.

The First Programmers

Yet women have a long history in computer science. Ada Lovelace wrote what is considered to be the first computer program in the 1840s, before computers as we know them even existed. Her program consisted of data inputs for a hypothetical machine called the Analytical Engine, designed by Charles Babbage. Though Babbage's machine was never built, his designs and Lovelace's ideas for how the machine could be used inspired those who eventually built the world's first computers.

In the 1940s, when the first electronic computers were finally built, the word "computer" was still a job title. It referred to a human, often a woman, who performed mathematical calculations. Six female mathematicians created programs for ENIAC, the world's first programmable general-purpose computer. Programming at the time was a tedious effort that involved punching cards with instructions in binary code. That would soon change, though, partially thanks to the efforts of another woman,

Grace Hopper. In the 1950s, she pioneered the development of programming languages written in English that would then be compiled into code the computer could read.

Women have contributed to computer science in other ways as well. In the 1960s, Margaret Hamilton wrote software that made the *Apollo 11* moon landing possible. This feat was even more incredible because software as a concept had just barely begun. Carol Shaw programmed video games in the 1970s, including the Atari hit *River Raid*. Anita Borg founded the Institute for Women and Technology, now known as the Anita Borg Institute, in 1994 to help support women in computing. When Evelyn Boyd Granville received a PhD in mathematics in 1949, she was the second black woman ever to achieve that honor. She worked for NASA and later became an educator. She said, "We accepted education as the means to rise above the limitations that a **prejudiced** society endeavored to place upon us."[8] Katherine Johnson, a black woman who worked at NASA for over thirty years, was awarded the Presidential Medal of Freedom in 2015. Her story and those of other women of color who worked behind the scenes at NASA is told in the January 2017 movie *Hidden Figures*.

Bryant's Role Models

Kimberly Bryant could point to any of these women as role models for herself and the girls in her program. However, when asked what person, living or dead, she would most like to have dinner with, she chose Martin Luther King Jr.[9] She added that the living person she would most like to meet would have to be Oprah Winfrey, the talk show star who hosted the wildly popular *Oprah Winfrey Show* from 1986 through 2011. Bryant says that Oprah has been with her all along her path, from the time she was growing up in Memphis. "Mother Oprah has an answer for anything you want to figure out in your life," she says. She points to a quote from Oprah, "Always take a stand for yourself, your values. You're defined by what you stand for."[10]

Kimberly Bryant chose to take a stand when she realized that even in 2011, the technology field was not diverse. Despite the monumental efforts of the activists of the civil rights and women's movements, technology was still mostly designed by white males. Bryant says:

We're missing out on the innovation, solutions, and creativity that a broader pool of talent can bring to the table. This really is an issue of social justice. It's about equaling and leveling the playing field for everyone.[11]

Just as Martin Luther King Jr. and others involved in the civil rights movement took a stand against unjust laws and unfair discrimination, Bryant is taking a stand for equal access to education in technology.

For Bryant, the revolution is far from over; it's just beginning.

Kimberly Bryant's Favorite Things:

Food: Thai or Mediterranean

Movie genre: Science fiction

Authors: Anne Rice and Stephen King

Programming language: Fortran

Apps: SoundCloud or Evernote

Instagram filter: Inkwell

Ideal vacation: A warm, sunny beach on the Caribbean

Best advice: Follow your passion

Something she does every day: Takes time in meditation or quiet prayer

CHAPTER TWO

Becoming an Electrical Engineer

T he Civil Rights Act made discrimination based on race or ethnicity illegal, and the women's movement opened up new opportunities in the workplace for women. But things were still far from equal in the 1980's. **Stereotypes** and discrimination continued to hamper the ability of women and people of color to succeed and follow

Kirkland Hall is one of the oldest and most prominent buildings at Vanderbilt University in Nashville, Tennessee.

their dreams. Yet as a student in high school, Kimberly Bryant experienced none of this. Her family, teachers, and others supported her and encouraged her, and she excelled. She took AP Calculus, AP English, AP Latin, and many other honors classes.

When her guidance counselors suggested pursuing an engineering degree, Bryant decided on civil engineering. Civil engineers design and maintain public structures such as bridges, dams, highways, energy systems, airports, and more. Bryant had always enjoyed social activism, so she wanted to pursue a type of engineering that would keep her close to the people, benefiting the community.

She was in for a rude awakening. At Vanderbilt University, she was one of just a handful of women in the engineering program, and one of only a few black people to boot. It was a difficult, lonely time. Bryant regularly faced discrimination. She admits that at times she was so unhappy there that she almost quit.

Culture Shock

Located in Nashville, Tennessee, Vanderbilt University is just a three-hour drive away from Memphis, where Bryant grew up. But it might as well have been a different country, or even a different planet. "It was like landing on Mars and trying to figure out my way," says Bryant.[1] While Memphis was a predominantly African American community, Vanderbilt was not.

Known as the "Harvard of the South," Vanderbilt was founded in 1874. Its Victorian Gothic architecture created an atmosphere of regal wealth and scholarly study. Massive buildings fronted with columns, ornate doorways, or wide stone steps presided over vast green lawns and pathways. It looked very different from the bustling city where Bryant had spent her childhood.

However, the biggest culture shock wasn't visual, it was emotional. During her childhood and teen years, Bryant had been a smart kid in a good school, surrounded by people who supported her. She received constant recognition for her achievements and encouragement to pursue her dreams. At Vanderbilt, she felt invisible. No one knew her and no one seemed to want to get to know her. At the same time, paradoxically, she felt much too visible. She stuck out due to the color of her skin and the fact that she was female.

An incident in one of her first classes illustrates what life was like for her in college. She was in a first-year civil engineering class with around one hundred other students. Yet as she recalls, she was the only student of color and one of just a few women. The professor asked how many students had taken an AP class and received a grade of three or higher on the test. Nobody raised their hand. "I looked around, and I slowly raised my hand," says Bryant.[2] But the professor ignored her. He didn't acknowledge that anyone had raised their hand. And he was the head of the civil engineering department. Bryant says:

I didn't know how to react to that. I was used to being lauded, to being encouraged. This was a totally different experience for me, and it was my first week of classes! I recognized without a doubt that it was going to take a lot for me to be able to survive in this environment.[3]

Finding a Mentor

Thinking back on that moment in her civil engineering class now, Bryant feels that the professor probably didn't believe it was possible that this black girl could have reached a higher level of achievement than all the white men sitting around her. "I don't think it registered in his mind that it could be a reality. So he wasn't able to recognize me," she says.[4] At the time, though, it was a crushing blow to her self-confidence. After a few weeks, she left the civil engineering program. She might have left school altogether if not for a chance meeting with an upperclassman.

While walking around campus one day, she ran into a tall, black woman. They started to talk, and the woman told Bryant that she was in the electrical engineering program. Bryant instantly started asking questions, and soon she began taking electrical engineering classes herself. "Seeing a young woman of color that was doing something I may be interested in—that made a difference," she says.[5] That woman mentored Bryant throughout her time at Vanderbilt and is still one of her closest friends. This experience is one reason why Black Girls Code emphasizes role models for the girls in the program. The group makes sure to bring in volunteers who are women of color so that the girls can see someone who looks like them working in **software engineering**, robotics, or another technical field.

Though having a mentor and other allies helped Bryant stay in school, she continued to struggle against discrimination. "Some of the perceptions from my professors were that I was less than, or that I wouldn't be able to compete, or wouldn't be able to meet the same bar as my peers," she says.[6] To put it bluntly, many of her professors and classmates thought she didn't belong in those engineering classrooms. The fact that she had attended a top high school and been an honor-roll student didn't matter. No one saw that at Vanderbilt. They only saw her gender and the color of her skin, and assumed she didn't belong. Bryant says:

> *Getting through Vanderbilt Engineering School was one of the hardest things I ever did in my life at the time—but it was also a great achievement. It gave me the grit and the resiliency to be able to stick to the path I'm on right now, regardless of what the roadblocks are. I'm sticking with it to make a difference.[7]*

Bryant hopes that the students participating in Black Girls Code never have to face the same roadblocks. She hopes that they will succeed or fail based on their own merits and natural abilities, and not because of anyone's preconceived notions about what girls or people of color can or can't do. "I want them to have that benefit of the doubt that they have the same skills, access, and opportunities as any other person,"[8] she says.

Working in Biotechnology

Despite the prejudices and **biases** Bryant faced in school, she obtained her degree and set out to begin her career. Though her experiences in the workforce weren't as difficult as her time in school, she was still often the only woman or person of color on her team. Early in her career, when one of her managers introduced her to the team, he said that they "'got a twofer,'" Bryant recalls, because she was a woman and a person of color.[9] He likely meant that the company had fulfilled some of its **diversity** goals by hiring her, but of course using that kind of language put Bryant on the spot and made it sound as if she'd been hired for her gender or the color of her skin rather than for her skills and experience. Though that manager overall is someone she admires, the way he talked about her reveals the kind of discrimination she regularly had to face during her career.

Bryant had focused on high-voltage electronics in a very important time period for the industry. Personal computers were just becoming common in people's homes. Engineering graduates had a plethora of career options and opportunities. In some positions, she did what she refers to as "hard-core engineering," such as climbing up a 200-foot (61-meter) gas tower in a hard hat, or walking around a factory wearing a respirator. In other positions, she worked at a desk on information technology, building software or working on databases.[10]

Her first job was as a sales engineer at Westinghouse Electric, a company that made and sold machinery used in the transmission and generation of electricity. A year later, she took a job as a plant supervisor at DuPont, a company that produces chemicals. She also worked for a few years at the tobacco company Philip Morris International before transitioning to the biomedical industry in the late 1990s.

She started at Merck, one of the world's largest manufacturers of medications and vaccines, in September 1998. There, she spent five years managing mechanical and maintenance workforces. Next, Bryant moved on to one of the medical industry's other giants: Pfizer. She worked there from 2004 through 2006, also managing maintenance operations and developing staffing solutions.

Though she was working with other engineers in a technical industry, Bryant hadn't stopped being a social activist. While at Merck, she worked on several diversity and inclusion programs. Leonie Wedderburn, who coordinated these programs with Bryant, says, "Kimberly has strong interpersonal skills, including tact, diplomacy, persuasion, cooperation and motivation."[11] Bryant also spent time supporting her local community. After moving out to San Francisco in 2006 for a job with the biomedical company Genentech, she joined the Middle Polk Neighborhood Association, an organization devoted to strengthening and beautifying the community in the San Francisco Bay Area.

The same year that Bryant started her new job, Genentech was named number one on *Fortune* magazine's list of the one hundred best companies to work for. The company, which developed new medical technology, focused on creating an environment where employees would enjoy coming to work every day— including a six-week paid sabbatical program, corporate childcare, a company-sponsored gym, and more. At Genentech, Bryant managed teams of programmers, data analysts, and computer support specialists. She was then promoted to a position as senior project manager and guided major IT initiatives through the development process. One of her colleagues at Genentech, Sandor Schoichet, says that he met Bryant when she took over management of a highly technical team in the middle of a critical systems infrastructure replacement project. "She came up to speed very quickly, and proved herself a decisive team leader and project manager," he says. "Kimberly succeeded in getting this project 'over the top' where a number of prior managers had failed."[12]

Ready for a Change

When Genentech went through a buyout in 2010, Kimberly Bryant took that as her cue to make a change in her career. "I was really burned out by the corporate grind, but I still loved what I was doing on the healthcare and **biotech** side," she says.[13] She had been paid well in her management positions and received a substantial package as part of the buyout. She intended to put her savings into a start-up business. Though she didn't have a specific idea in mind, she knew she wanted to help people. She thought she'd do something technology related that involved solving critical health-care problems.

As she toyed with different ideas for her business, she spent time volunteering for organizations such as the Institute for OneWorld Health, a nonprofit drug development organization that worked on medications to treat diseases in developing nations. The organization is now part of global health nonprofit PATH. Her supervisor at OneWorld Health, Amanda L'Esperance, says, "You can tell a lot about a person's character based on how they perform as a volunteer." She says that Kimberly was motivated, self-directed, well organized, and a pleasure to be around.[14]

Genentech may very well have been the best place to work in the United States. But that didn't mean the company had completely overcome discrimination and bias. At her job, industry conferences, and later at networking events and meet-ups, Bryant often experienced a feeling of déjà vu, as if she were back in that college civil engineering class. She was often the only female and almost always the only black female in the room. Even though it wasn't as common for people to discredit her, she still felt like an outsider. It had been over twenty years since she'd graduated from Vanderbilt, yet the tech industry still wasn't very inclusive.

Something was wrong, but Bryant didn't yet know that she would be the one to do something about it. Her revolutionary idea was just beginning to take hold.

Student Communities

While at Vanderbilt, Kimberly Bryant relied on the African American student community for support. At the time she attended school, African Americans made up only about 1 to 3 percent of the student population. Thankfully, the Bishop Joseph Johnson Black Cultural Center, affectionately known as "The House," provided a place where she could go to hang out, study, and connect with others who had a similar background and were facing similar experiences. The center was established in 1984 in honor of Bishop Joseph A. Johnson Jr., the first African American to graduate from Vanderbilt. Today, the center organizes and presents speakers, panel discussions, book clubs, plays, musical performances, and more. Many colleges and universities in the United States are home to similar student organizations devoted to providing support to minority communities on campus.

CHAPTER THREE

Inspiration Strikes

Kimberly Bryant never wanted to start a nonprofit. In fact, she has called herself an "accidental nonprofit **entrepreneur**."[1] She fully intended to found her own business in biotechnology. But two experiences coincided to convince her that she had to change her plans. First, at conferences and networking events, she kept hearing people ask why there weren't enough women working in technology. Second, she noticed a startling lack of diversity at a computer science camp that her daughter attended. She decided that it was up to her to do something.

Kimberly Bryant hopes that one day it will be commonplace to find women and people of color working in technology classrooms, conferences, and companies.

The Only One in the Room

In order to start a business and find support and funding, an entrepreneur needs to network and meet lots of people. So after leaving her corporate job in 2010, Bryant started attending events in the San Francisco Bay Area related to technology, women entrepreneurs, and more, such as the Berkeley Women Entrepreneurs Conference. At event after event, she noticed that there were often no other women or people of color. In addition, she kept hearing questions and conversations about the lack of women working in technology. Some people suggested that the problem was due to a shortage of women who were interested in tech careers. Others pointed to a dwindling pipeline, in which girls and women drop out of science and technology along the way from middle school to high school to college and finally to the workforce.

At first, Bryant was simply perplexed. She didn't understand how it could be possible that nothing had changed in terms of diversity in technology since she had graduated with her degree in electrical engineering and computer science in 1989. This was especially troubling given that the information technology industry was growing so rapidly, and Silicon Valley was at the heart of the explosion. Yet even there, she was surrounded by a crowd of almost entirely white men.

Her confusion gradually morphed into frustration. She remembers thinking, "Twenty-plus years after

I received my engineering degree, and we're still complaining that we can't find women to fill these roles. It's ridiculous."[2] Finally, frustration gave way to a sense of determination. She recalls one panel discussion in which someone asked a question about women in technology. The panelist answered that women were just not going into engineering or computer science. Bryant says:

> *I kept hearing this ... that we were not rising up to lead or found these companies. I vividly remember sitting in that room thinking, "I have to do something, because I don't want to hear anyone give that response again."*[3]

A Mother's Horror

However, Bryant wasn't frustrated and determined enough yet to abandon her plans to start a biotechnology business. The turning point came in 2010 after she sent her daughter, Kai Morton, to summer camp. This wasn't your normal summer camp—it was a course in game design at Stanford University. Kai, who was eleven at the time, had always loved science and technology. As a little girl, she had preferred LEGOs to Barbies and Gameboys to tea sets. By middle school, Kai was heavily into gaming, even though she was the only one in her circle of friends who was into such "geeky stuff," says Bryant.[4] "The kid was wed to the computer like it was her Siamese twin. I did not understand why you would spend all your time and waking hours playing a game, but she did."[5] Kai especially enjoyed World of Warcraft.

Yet Kai had no concept that technology could be used for creation and not just consumption. She thought it might be cool to work as a game tester but hadn't considered working as a game programmer. Attending that Stanford summer camp did the trick. Kai's whole perspective changed. An interest in game design and programming flourished, and she decided she wanted to attend Stanford. In the summer of 2011, she returned to attend Stanford's Digital Media Academy. She got the game-themed nickname "Zelda," after a famous game character, and learned even more about designing and programming video games. In a blog post reflecting on the experience, she writes, "I thought that I could make a game just like my favorite game World of Warcraft [WoW], but then I realized that World of Warcraft is a really hard game to make. So I am trying to make my way up to my ultimate goal of creating a game like WoW."[6]

Kai was loving programming, but there was one big problem. At the end of the 2010 camp, the kids put on a presentation for their parents. While Bryant was watching, she noticed that in the group of around thirty-five students, there were only a few girls and no other students of color. Kai's class looked almost exactly the same as Bryant's freshman class at Vanderbilt. Then, in the car ride home, Kai told her mom that the instructors hadn't paid very much attention to the girls in the classroom.

Bryant was horrified. "It crushed my soul to the core," she says.[7] She couldn't believe Kai was facing the same non-inclusive environment that she had as an engineering student. While she was proud that her daughter seemed poised to follow in her footsteps as an engineer, she was also terrified that Kai would have to walk the same treacherous path that she had. Bryant says:

Some of the things I experienced were really scary, and they weren't experiences that I wanted for my daughter ... I wanted her to have an easier and more enjoyable time doing the thing that she loves.[8]

She didn't want her daughter to experience discrimination or unfair stereotypes. She also worried that her daughter would feel culturally isolated. Would Kai give up on her passions if she never saw any other girls or people of color in her classrooms? Bryant herself almost had. She was determined to find a way to provide her daughter with a network of support. "When I tell the story of Black Girls Code, I'm also telling the story of a mother," Bryant says.[9] She was doing something to make the world a better place for her child.

Black Girls Code is Born

At first, Bryant thought she would just take some of her savings and send ten girls to the camp at Stanford the next summer. But as she told people about her plan, they started suggesting that she create her own camp instead. The idea was daunting, but Bryant gradually realized that it was the best thing to do if she really wanted a better future for her daughter. She set out to create a program that would nurture girls like Kai, and Black Girls Code was born.

To Bryant, the program was always about much more than just teaching girls how to write computer code. From the beginning, it was all about revolutionizing the way the world sees women and people of color, and making a more welcoming space for them in technology. She wanted to create a movement to bring girls like Kai together. She envisioned a "community of little black and brown girls that are geeky, very into gaming, like to spend time on the computer, and are doing robotics."[10] Instead of being alone on their journeys through their educations and careers, these girls would have a whole tribe of others to support and validate them.

At first, Bryant didn't know what to call her organization. She wrote down a lot of ideas, including "Kaleidoscope Girls," but none seemed just right. One day, she wrote down "Black Girls Code." At first, the name seemed like it might be too radical—she thought maybe no one would accept it. So she sat on it for a long time. One problem was that she didn't want minorities who weren't African American to feel that they weren't welcome.

While she was worrying about the name, Bryant attended the 2011 BlogHer Business, Entrepreneurism and Technology conference. There, she watched a presentation by Analisa Balares, the founder of Womensphere, an organization devoted to unleashing the leadership potential of women and girls around the world. After the presentation, Bryant went up to Balares and showed her the name. She told Bryant to pull out her phone right now and claim the domain name for the website. As Bryant recalls, "She said, 'I connect with this name. I am a black girl, too.'"[11] Balares was Filipino, but the name was still meaningful to her. Bryant realized that blackness as a concept could transcend multiple cultures.

Still, some people criticize the name, saying that it's too exclusionary. In fact, Black Girls Code welcomes girls of all ethnicities, and occasionally hosts mixed-gender events. In addition, Bryant points out that plenty of other programs on coding and technology focus on girls in general or on young people, including boys. However, Bryant believes strongly that it's important for girls of color to have a program that focuses on them. If the program were open to everyone, many of the girls might not want to be there. It might turn into just another technology club for geeky boys, with a few token girls and kids of color.

To Bryant and her supporters, the name "Black Girls Code" is a bold, empowering statement. It's an affirmation that makes it very clear that coding is something that women of color do. "[The girls] latch on immediately and take a lot of pride in the name," she says. They realize that the program is meant to support them specifically. Then they meet mentors in the program that look like them, and they start to thrive, flourish, and blossom, says Bryant.[12]

In April 2011, she launched the organization. In her very first blog post on the new website, she wrote that young people of color need to see role models who look like themselves working in **STEM** fields. (STEM stands for "science, technology, engineering, and math.") Currently, the role models people think of in technology are people such as Bill Gates, founder of Microsoft, Steve Jobs, who cofounded Apple, or Mark Zuckerberg, founder of Facebook, all of whom are white men. Girls and kids of color need to see themselves reflected in these roles in order to believe that success is possible and to also feel like working in tech might be a cool thing to do. Bryant wrote:

> *I founded Black Girls Code with the specific goal of creating opportunities for girls of color to envision themselves as the "masters of their technological universe." I am in search of the next (Black) Mark Zuckerberg. Above all I am hopeful that she will forge a new pathway towards innovation and social impact that will change the equation for future generations of black and brown creators and leaders in technology. It is a mission that is long overdue.*[13]

The First Workshop

To get Black Girls Code started, Kimberly Bryant paid out of her own pocket. Her original team included two of Bryant's friends and former colleagues from Genentech.

They were both moms, and one of them had a science background and had formerly been a middle school teacher. Then, at a Code for America meeting one night, Bryant passed around that she had cut out of cardboard, and she managed to get the attention of a man who was on a fellowship to spend a year using his technical skills to better local communities and governments. He was the only real coder on the team, Bryant recalls, and they relied heavily on his skills and experience. "Although we may have been lacking in numbers and been slight newbies in the coding skills, we made up for these deficiencies with our passion and dedication," Bryant says.[14]

The group put together a six-week-long pilot program of workshops centered on computer science and coding. They decided to hold the classes in a San Francisco community called Bayview-Hunters Point. Though the tech revolution has increased the wealth and prosperity of much of Silicon Valley, Bayview-Hunters Point is one of the areas that got left behind. In this mainly black community, extreme poverty, pollution, and gang violence plague residents. The area is located just outside of Genentech, and the company had done outreach work in the area. So Bryant and her friends knew that there was a need in this community. In addition, they knew they'd be able to reach their target group of girls of color.

Bryant and her friends started out by talking to the local YWCA to look for a space for their workshop. Then they found a nonprofit organization with computer lab space in the basement. The room only had six workstations, so they set a goal of finding six middle school girls for the pilot program. Bryant's research had shown that middle school is a critical time for girls—it's during those years that the percentage of girls who are interested in a career in technology drops drastically. But at the first parent information night about the new program, many moms and dads brought younger siblings along. Some were as young as six or seven. The group didn't have any strict rules yet for Black Girls Code, so they welcomed the elementary-school-aged kids along with their middle-school-aged sisters. They wound up with twelve girls in that first class, including Bryant's daughter Kai as well as children of the other founders. "They were like our guinea pigs,"[15] Bryant says.

As Bryant's team was securing a space and recruiting students, they were also searching for the perfect tool to use to teach coding to young students. They took their "guinea pigs" and a few other interested students to LEGO Mindstorms robotics classes, a Silicon Valley Code Camp at Hills College in San Francisco, and a KidsRuby class at the Golden Gate Ruby Conference in San Francisco. Nailah, who was seven years old, attended the KidsRuby class. She didn't know what to expect. Afterwards, she said, "This was my very first time learning how to program and I had a really fun experience … What I liked the most was that I could learn to hack my homework!"[16] By that, she meant that she could now write a computer program to solve a certain kind of math problem, instead of doing every single math problem by hand. Kai also attended the KidsRuby class. She described the experience as fun, interesting, and informative. The teacher would throw candy to kids who answered his questions correctly. "I got so much candy that after a while the teacher asked somebody else to answer a question! I saved all the candy till the end and gobbled it all down,"[17] she said.

Bryant's team eventually settled on Scratch as the tool they would use in their first workshop. Scratch is a free tool designed by the MIT Media Lab to teach young people about programming concepts such as loops, events, conditional operators, variables, and more. Finally, the six-week program got underway, holding the first class in October 2011. Bryant admits that some of the girls resisted the **curriculum** at first. They told her they would rather be out with their friends at the mall. But by the end of the two-and-a-half-hour class, the kids all started to see that technology could be really interesting. In fact, the girls regularly outran the curriculum. Bryant and the other instructors would often have to scramble to find something else for the students to do. In addition, they noticed that the younger girls excelled at the material. They could do a lot of the same work as the older girls and tended to be more enthusiastic about it, too.

Originally, Bryant and her team hadn't planned to hold another session until March of 2012. But that first Black Girls Code workshop garnered so much interest that they added a session for younger girls in January 2012. In addition, a company called ThoughtWorks reached out to the new organization to ask how they could help. "That's when we started to grow our program throughout the Bay Area and beyond," says Bryant.[18] ThoughtWorks helped fund and coordinate events in cities including Dallas, New York, and Chicago. They also helped open a chapter in Johannesburg, South Africa, in 2012. In addition, Google provided an early seed grant to help Black Girls Code grow.

Now, Kimberly Bryant has no regrets about giving up her biotechnology start-up dream in order to found a nonprofit. "It's nowhere near as lucrative as biotech, but it is one of the most rewarding things I've ever done in my career,"[19] she says. Black Girls Code has become the revolution Bryant once dreamed about.

Meet Kai

Kai Morton was just twelve years old when her mother founded Black Girls Code. By seventeen, she learned six languages in addition to English—Java, JavaScript, HTML/CSS, Python, Swift, and Ruby and began learning Unity and Objective-C. All of those are programming languages used in web development, application development, or game development. Kai is still an avid gamer, though these days she's more into *League of Legends* and *Halo* than *World of Warcraft*. However, her interests go beyond technology and games. She's on her school's golf and track teams and plays bass guitar in a band.

Though Kai had originally hoped to attend Stanford, she now has her sights set on MIT. She participates in her high school robotics team and has developed her own app, She2U, which won second place in the 2015 pitch contest at Enza Academy, a youth innovation program at Stanford University. The app is a social network to help colleges and universities recruit female athletes. In 2016, *Teen Vogue* magazine named Kai one of their 21 under 21. This group of young women leaders includes social activists, athletes, inventors, artists, and coders like Kai. In the future, Kai hopes to become CEO of her own technology business, perhaps in video gaming. She's also proud of her mom's accomplishments. "When I grow older I really hope to make as much impact on the world as she does," she says.[20]

CHAPTER FOUR

Black Girls Code!

K imberly Bryant's decision to start Black Girls Code has affected the lives of thousands of young women. If not for the program, these students may never have discovered a love for coding or found mentors to guide them along a career path. Though it's only been six years since Black Girls Code launched, success stories abound about teens and young women who have moved on from the program to pursue a career in technology or engineering.

On its surface, Black Girls Code is an educational program that teaches coding languages, app development,

Black Girls Code students celebrate the 2016 opening of a new space for their group located in Google's offices in New York City.

game development, and robotics. Its specific mission is to deliver this education to girls ages seven to seventeen from underrepresented communities. But the true impact of the program goes far deeper. In addition to just teaching technical skills, the group also empowers girls with leadership skills and provides access to role models and mentoring in a supportive environment.

From San Francisco to South Africa

Since that first workshop in Bayview-Hunters Point, which focused on Scratch, Black Girls Code has continued to offer six-week-long after-school courses in a variety of technical subjects, including Ruby, Python, HTML/CSS, and mobile app development. The organization has also expanded its repertoire of events. Some popular one-day programs include: Build a Webpage in a Day, Build a Mobile App in a Day, Game Jam, and Robot Expo. These events bring girls together for six hours, usually on a Saturday, to create something using technology. The group also began hosting two-day girls-only hackathons in 2014. A hackathon is an event in which teams work together to create mobile applications or other software to solve a specific problem. These events usually offer prizes for the best application designs. In the summers, Black Girls Code holds week-long day camps in computer science. The camps combine concepts taught in the other programs. In order to get more Latino students involved, the group has also hosted workshops in both Spanish and English.

Black Girls Code chapters located all around the United States host these events throughout the year. San Francisco remains the organization's home base, but local chapters have opened in Atlanta, Boston, Chicago, Dallas, Los Angeles, Memphis, Miami, New York, Raleigh-Durham, and Washington, DC, as well as the one in Johannesburg, South Africa.

In addition to hosting its own events, Black Girls Code also regularly sends teams of girls to participate in other events, such as hackathons or conferences related to coding, leadership, women's rights, or minority rights. Of course, Kimberly Bryant can't be in more than one place at a time. A huge network of employees and volunteers run all of the local chapters. Meanwhile, Bryant spends much of her time traveling from place to place, making appearances at Black Girls Code workshops, speak at conferences and universities, and attending events related to technology, leadership, and empowerment.

Inside the Classroom

Despite the myriad locations and varied types of workshops offered, every Black Girls Code class or event has a few things in common. A student-to-teacher ratio of three to one or even two to one ensures that the students get lots of individual attention. Some of the teachers are professional educators, while others are experts working in a technical field at a corporation such as Google or Twitter. Black Girls Code trains these experts to deliver the classes. But some of the teachers are volunteers who act more as coaches to support and encourage the girls. Bryant explains that it's not necessary for all of the adults in the room to be experts. "We're teaching [the girls] how to learn as opposed to telling them everything to do," she says.[1]

In order to keep students engaged in the material, the curriculum is always project-based. The kids spend a minimal amount of time listening to a teacher talk. They aren't just learning how to code; they're actually using code to build something. "We lecture in small chunks and really make sure that our workshops are focused on the doing, the creating, the inquiry that comes from the students working on a project and asking questions of the mentors and teachers," says Bryant.[2] The classes revolve around creating a product that is fun, creative, or interesting, such as a video game or an app that addresses a social issue.

At a Black Girls Code Robot Expo held at Georgia Tech in Atlanta in 2016, the girls used LEGO kits to build and program robots. Some made spinning or motion-detecting bots. Others made a chomping alligator. During the process, they learned troubleshooting, revision, and creativity. Sarah Oso, a student at Georgia Tech, was one of the volunteer teachers at the event. She says she wasn't there to provide instruction or solutions. Rather, she supervised while the girls worked through each problem on their own. Oso says:

> *There is something lovely and powerful about the moment that lightbulb goes off and they discover an answer themselves—it's part of the learning process, and that's what they take home with them. I like getting to see that.*[3]

Bryant has found that girls prefer to collaborate— if given a choice, they almost always want to work on a team or with a partner—so the students often do pair programming. This is a technique in which two coders work together at one computer. One writes the code, while the other reviews each line. Every couple of minutes, the two swap roles. Not only do the students enjoy working in pairs, it also helps them learn that coding can be a social activity. The idea that coders are reclusive and spend a lot of time alone at a computer is one of the stereotypes Black Girls Code is turning on its head.

Nurturing Future Leaders and Creators

In addition to the technical curriculum, Black Girls Code workshops and events teach entrepreneurship, focusing on leadership and business skills girls need in order to start and run their own companies. Kimberly Bryant points out that her goals go beyond just getting more girls and people of color into software engineering roles at companies like Google. Instead, she wants to nurture students who will create the next Google or become the next Mark Zuckerberg. Her students have taken this

Sisters Jayda Ostrun (*left*) and Jessica Ostrun (*right*) participate in a Black Girls Code app-building workshop in New York in 2013.

lofty vision to heart. "Tech is gonna take over the world. I wanna be a part of that!" said thirteen-year-old Natalia Cox after attending a Black Girls Code summer camp in San Francisco in 2015.[4]

But before a girl like Natalia can build an app or a company that will change the world, she has to realize that such a thing is possible. Kimberly Bryant finds that many young black girls view technology in much the same way her daughter Kai once did—as consumers, not creators. In fact, Bryant often has to tell girls to put their phones away during workshops and classes! They use their smartphones all day long to play games, text friends, and take pictures, but they don't realize what's going on behind the scenes to make the device work. Very young kids actually need to learn that apps and games don't just magically exist—someone created them. Older kids and teens need to learn that it doesn't take a genius to create an app. They can build their own applications and games instead of always downloading them from the app store.

To help reinforce Black Girls Code's message about leadership, the group does a unity chant and pledge before opening up their computers. The girls all recite together, "I am going to be the creator of tomorrow."[5] Bryant says, "We are hoping to teach our girls to be builders and not just consumers. We need to teach our girls to solve problems, hack the issues that are important to them and their world."[6] This is important because the app a girl wants or needs doesn't always exist; she may have to create it herself. People who create technology choose what to create based on the needs they see in their lives or their communities. Sandra Horne, a staff member at Black Girls Code, says:

Learning to code is like holding the key to endless possibilities in technology. Coding turns people into creators, where they can make their own worlds and in turn promote a positive, sustainable change. That's the message we aim to send with each session here at Black Girls Code.[7]

In Kimberly Bryant's experience, girls and women tend to lean toward addressing social issues with their projects more than boys and men do. They often don't just aim to make a time-saving app or fun game; they try to make something that will result in social change. Black Girls Code encourages this and designs its curriculum around a purpose. The organization also sends teams to compete in events with themes related to social activism. The girls will often be tasked with building something that focuses on their community. For example, a team of Bryant's students designed an app called Ohana that would allow girls in crisis to alert the police in order to help prevent abductions. The app was one of three finalists at an international hackathon. Students from the program have also designed a recycling app and an app to make it easier for food banks to distribute food. In a keynote address at Vanderbilt University during National Engineers Week in 2014, Bryant challenged the engineers in the room to think of their role "as not just the makers of things but as the creators of social change."[8]

When a young person views herself (or himself) as a leader and a change agent, she builds self-confidence and **self-efficacy**. She starts to believe in her ability to succeed and believe that others will accept her as a leader. Bryant has seen this transformation again and again in her students. She likes to cite the African proverb "When you teach a woman, you teach a nation."[9] Her girls often use what they've learned to turn around and teach others.

One student, Aita, got caught teaching her friend at school how to build a website, so her teacher asked her to teach a series of workshops so even more students could learn. Aita was in middle school at the time. Bryant says, "These girls are developing confidence, self-advocacy, and strong leadership skills as a result of this affirmation that they are the leaders we've all been waiting for."[10] Holding on to that confidence, though, requires consistent support, especially from older mentors and role models.

A Mirror of Herself

Ideally, these mentors and role models should look like the young person or come from a similar background. Sharing gender, resemblance, hometown, or culture with another person creates an instant connection and helps build trust and familiarity. Back Girls Code purposefully recruits volunteers who are female, black, Latino, American Indian, or come from the girls' home city, and are currently working as engineers or in a technology-related field. Over two thousand volunteers have given their time to the organization. It helps that people with these backgrounds are drawn to work with Black Girls Code. When Kimberly Bryant put out a call for engineers in Silicon Valley to volunteer with her program, over 90 percent of the respondents were women. She hadn't requested female volunteers specifically, but clearly these women saw themselves reflected in the girls in the program.

In addition to the mentors who supervise classroom activities, Black Girls Code camps and workshops often include field trips to visit local technology companies or other relevant organizations, such as IBM, NASA, or the Computer Science Museum in Mountainview, California. On the last day of a 2013 Black Girls Code summer camp in Oakland, California, the students took a trip to the Facebook campus. They met with employees at Facebook, including Lauryn Hale, a strategic partnership developer who is African American. She said, "I think it's really awesome that Black Girls Code is here today. I know when I was their age, I wish I had the same type of opportunity and access to visit companies like this."[11]

Of course, many of the teachers, volunteers, and hosts at Black Girls Code events are white, male, or both—the organization certainly wouldn't exclude a qualified instructor on the basis of race or gender. In fact, volunteers from different backgrounds can connect to the girls in other ways that are also inspiring. Perhaps the volunteer faced similar hurdles due to poverty. On that same trip to Facebook, intern Jorge Cueto told the girls, "My family couldn't afford to have our own computer at home until I was a freshman in high school. I only started [programming] last summer and I'm already interning at Facebook. I think it's definitely something anyone can do."[12] Facebook Chief Operating Officer Sheryl Sandberg also talked to the group. She spoke

Former first lady Michelle Obama has been an important role model for many children, and especially for girls of color.

about the need for more women to learn programming skills in order to become future leaders.

Although anyone can provide an inspiration to a young person, a role model who is the same gender, same race, or from the same neighborhood makes that moment of connection and inspiration inevitable. "You need to see yourself, a reflection of yourself, to build self-confidence," says Bryant.[13]

It can be difficult for members of the dominant culture to understand the importance of this mirror. But for women and minorities, it's a big deal. Coder Sasha Williams was 14 when she helped create the Ohana app. She started attending Black Girls Code events when she was in middle school. At the time, she was one of maybe five African Americans attending her school in Concord, California. She explains that she likes going to Black Girls Code for several reasons, including the fact that she can see girls who look like her. Williams's three main heroes, Michelle Obama, Oprah Winfrey, and her mom, demonstrate the importance of strong role models who are both female and black. There's a reason that Williams and other black girls don't usually point to people like Mark Zuckerberg as a personal hero. He doesn't seem like someone Williams could grow up to be, but Michelle Obama does. Becky Blalock, a retired Chief Information Officer who wrote a book about how women can reach the highest levels of leadership, says, "It is very hard to be something you have never seen."[14]

When There's No Computer at Home

Being able to create using technology requires more than just an education, self-confidence, and role models. As Cueto pointed out, kids also need access to a computer. Smartphones, tablets, and computers are becoming more and more widespread every year, but in low-income communities, it's often rare for a child to have a computer at home. Even scarier, that child may not have access to a computer at school, either. The school may not have enough equipment, or its equipment could be ten or twenty years old and out of date. In one of the communities Bryant visited in San Francisco, the school had Macintosh computers that came out in 1985 for the kids to learn on. And that school was in the middle of Silicon Valley! Broadband or wireless internet access is an issue as well.

Kimberly Bryant says access to computers and the internet is one of her students' biggest obstacles. "We may have a hundred girls in a class," she says, "but probably only a quarter of them have access to a laptop. It's hard to engage them in learning when they don't have access to the equipment to continue to develop their skill sets."[15] To help handle this issue, the group sometimes gives out kits with Scratch or another programming tool to allow the girls to continue to practice on their own.

Another important way to keep kids engaged after the class, workshop, or camp is over is to get parents involved. During that first workshop in 2011, Bryant noticed that parents were very concerned about what their daughters were doing, so she had the parents come in and watch their daughters put on a presentation. From there, the organization kept offering ways for parents to participate. Now, most of their workshops include either an activity or presentation for parents, or even parallel classes where they learn the same topics as their daughters. That way, the parents are better equipped to provide support and encouragement at home. "Parents are some of the strongest advocates for the students," says Bryant. "If we can get them on board, we know the student is more likely to stay in the program."[16] And Black Girls Code students are very likely to stick with the program. More than 75 percent of the girls participating in events have attended before.

The Girl Scouts of Technology

Bryant is looking into creating a badge system similar to the one used by the Girl Scouts to help students track their progress and celebrate their successes. In fact, Bryant wants her organization to become known as "the Girl Scouts of technology."[17] By that, she means that she wants Black Girls Code to be as widespread, well known, and well respected as the Girl Scouts.

The girls and their families are the ones helping to spread the word about the organization. When they return to attend a second or third workshop, they usually bring their friends. Bryant and her team also perform outreach in the communities they serve to recruit new students, but they don't have to do a lot of advertising. Excitement about their events spreads quickly via word of mouth. Events are so popular that they often sell out.

While it does cost money to attend a Black Girls Code event, the organization offers scholarships to make it easier for girls from low-income communities to participate. As of 2014, around 90 percent of the girls who had attended camps and workshops didn't have to pay. The money for scholarships and day-to-day operations comes mainly from corporate sponsorships. Companies such as Google, Adobe, and Verizon help support Black Girls Code programs by contributing food, space, equipment, or money. In addition, fundraising campaigns help gather individual contributions. In 2013, Kimberly Bryant and her team kicked off a campaign on Indiegogo to raise money for a Summer of Code. The money would help bring their program to ten new cities, help establish new local chapters, and fund a web video series about their work. They exceeded their goal of $100,000 and raised $114,840. Supporters got Black Girls Code buttons, wristbands, water bottles, T-shirts, and more as appreciation for their contributions.

By 2016, Black Girls Code had become popular enough to earn a cameo appearance on the hit Fox TV show *Empire*. The show is a drama set in New York about hip hop music artists and record labels. In an episode that aired on October 5, 2016, one of the main characters, Cookie Lyon, gets shown around a Black Girls Code seminar. Her guide, a wealthy lawyer named Angelo Dubois, tells her, "This is the future, this right here. This is how we rise."[18]

Kimberly Bryant completely agrees with that sentiment. She was showered with tweets congratulating

Black Girls Code and bearing the hashtag #howwerise. Bryant and her Black Girls Code workshops have inspired many people of all different backgrounds. But when asked what inspires her, Bryant says that it's the girls who attend her programs.

What I see in them that really touches me the most is their bravery. Their bravery to step out and do something that they may be unfamiliar with, that they didn't know before, and use that as a lever to grow their self-confidence, their self-efficacy. But it started with them just being brave enough to say: "I want to learn." [19]

Ohana

During the IGNITE International Girls Hackathon event in February 2015, the Global Fund for Women challenged coders to design websites or mobile apps that would help increase girls' access to safe spaces in their communities. Teams participated from all over the world, including the United States, Taiwan, India, and Brazil. A Black Girls Code team out of Oakland, California, entered the competition. Kimberly Bryant's daughter, Kai, was on the team, along with Sasha Williams and three other girls. The called their app Ohana, a Hawaiian word that was popularized by the Disney movie *Lilo and Stitch*, which includes the line, "Ohana means family, and family means no one gets left behind or forgotten."

The Ohana app prompts a user to set up contacts and compose messages to be sent in case of emergency. The user can update her status to either green for safe, orange for unsure or upset, or red for danger. In case she doesn't have access to her phone in an emergency, she can place a tiny sensor onto a piece of jewelry or a zipper. When she holds down the sensor for five seconds, the app automatically changes the status to red and sends an alert to the police and the emergency contacts. The app uses GPS tracking to send the user's location as well. The designers hope that the app will help prevent sexual harassment, domestic violence, and abductions.

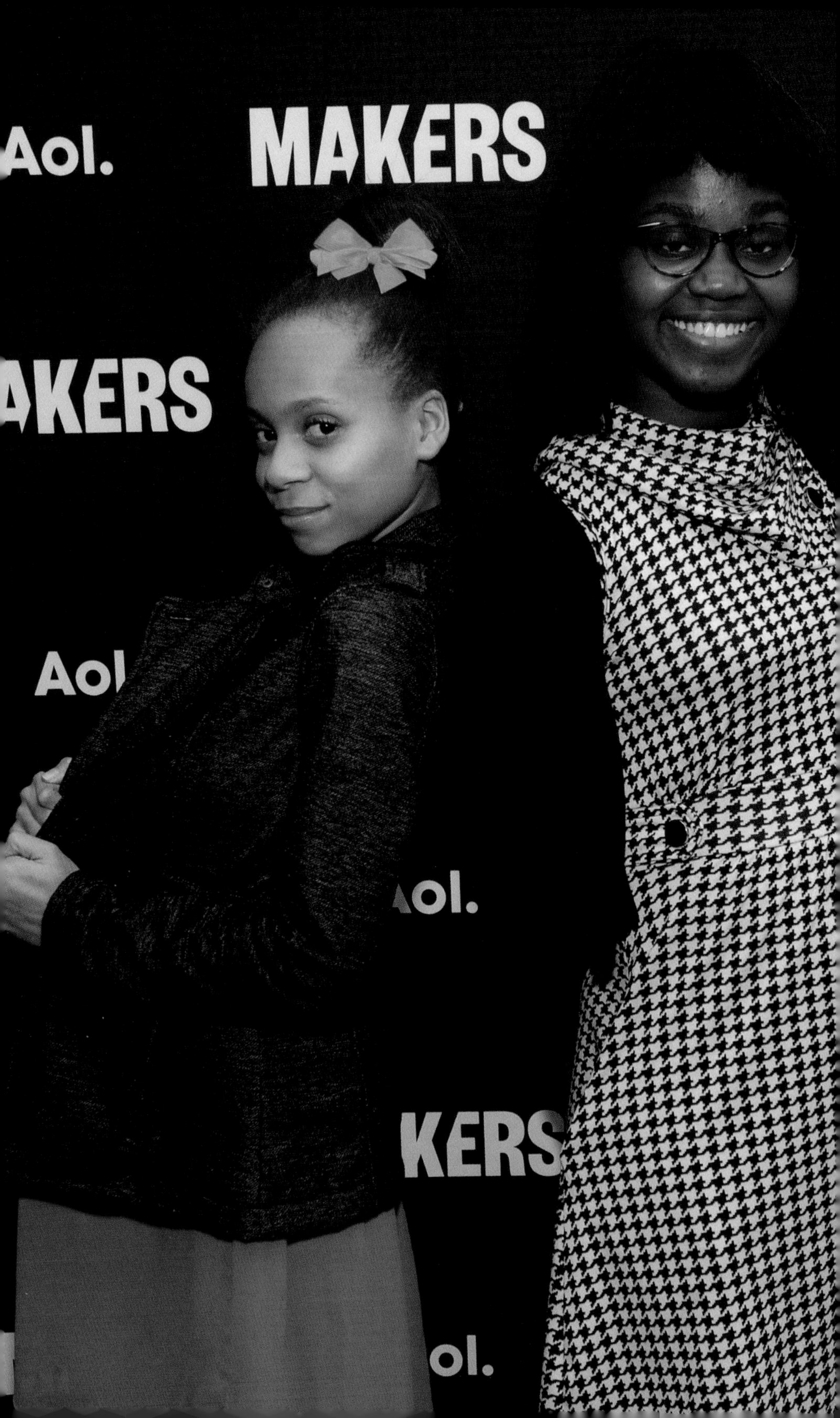
Aol.
MAKERS
AKERS
Aol
Aol.
KERS
ol.

CHAPTER FIVE

Fighting for Diversity

K imberly Bryant's Black Girls Code workshops and events teach kids how to program. That alone might be considered revolutionary, especially since many schools still lack the faculty and resources to teach this essential skill. But there are plenty of other nonprofits out there promoting education in computer science and coding. Bryant's real revolution is to nurture a generation of girls of color who will become leaders in technology. She's striving to change a cultural paradigm in which women and people of color are often not encouraged or expected to achieve greatness, especially

Students from Black Girls Code regularly attend events that promote technology, diversity, and women's empowerment, including the 2016 Makers Conference in California.

not in the fields of science and technology. "Having women of color at the forefront and being key participants in learning this skill set is revolutionary," says Bryant.[1] As a social activist, Kimberly Bryant focuses on the issue of increasing diversity in the technology workforce.

Carol Fife, a volunteer for Black Girls Code and mother of a participant, says that in a literal sense, the girls are learning how to code web pages and write programs for robots. "But figuratively I think it's a way that we move forward into the future with how we do things, how we innovate, and how we bring our essence back to dominant culture. Because right now our narrative is kind of left out of the story."[2] Fife and others in the organization envision a future in which it's no longer rare to find a black, Latina, or American Indian woman working in computer science, engineering, or other STEM fields.

To help make this future a reality, Kimberly Bryant regularly speaks out about diversity, women's rights, and rights for minorities. She speaks at conferences and media events, including the Personal Democracy Forum, TEDx Kansas City, InspireFest, and the Big Ideas Festival. She's also given a keynote address about diversity at Vanderbilt University. Through these speaking engagements, she spreads the word about her organization and about the cultural biases that she's trying to turn upside down. When she sees girls from her program succeed, she says, "I like to think that they are bending the stereotype of what it means to be a coder and what impact coding could have on our world."[3] She believes that these girls will transform the technology industry to become more diverse and inclusive.

Dangerous Misconceptions

Many people think that the reason for the lack of women and people of color in technology is that these groups simply aren't interested in that career, that they'd rather do something else with their lives. Other people go so far as to make the sexist argument that girls aren't smart enough to learn math or computer science, or the racist argument that says the same thing about young people of color. These are all extremely troubling misconceptions because race and gender have nothing to do with a person's innate intelligence or ability to learn.

A 2010 report from the American Association of University Women looked for reasons why men outnumber women in STEM fields. Their conclusion was that the problem was not related to aptitude or ability. Rather, societal beliefs and educational environments greatly impacted girls' achievements. For example, a girl who regularly hears or experiences the stereotype that boys are better at math is going to have lower expectations for herself and is actually likely to perform worse on tests of her abilities. Research has shown that when a class is told that boys and girls are equally likely to do well in math, tests show no difference in average scores by

The character Sheldon Cooper (*right*) of the popular television sitcom *Big Bang Theory* personifies the stereotypes about the kind of person who enjoys science, engineering, and technology.

gender. The report says that girls self-report lower math skills than boys who have similar achievement levels. This results in girls feeling less capable of succeeding in fields that require math, such as engineering or computer science. "A lot of girls feel like they're not supposed to be involved in technology—that's a guy thing," says Emily Watt, a Black Girls Code participant.[4]

The 2015 documentary *Code: Debugging the Gender Gap*, directed by Robin Hauser Reynolds, opens with a scene showing seventh- and eighth-grade students describing what a computer programmer looks like. Some of their answers include: glasses, nerdy, a man. Finally, one girl says, "I guess it could also be a woman."[5] Yet the image of a young, white, male geek sitting alone at a computer persists throughout popular culture. That is not a welcoming image for everyone, says Bryant. Plus, it's not true! While women and people of color may be underrepresented in technology, they are definitely out there.

The Pipeline Problem

In elementary school, boys and girls express an interest in science and scientific careers in roughly equal numbers. But in middle and high school, the number of girls who want to stick with science, engineering, and technology plummets. It's during this time period that stereotypes about girls' abilities and perceptions about technology as uncool start to take hold. For that reason, Bryant's organization tries to capture girls' interest early, with programs for kids as young as seven. If young girls aren't given the encouragement that they can do technical work and it's cool to do it, Bryant says, they start to opt out. And they keep opting out and dropping out all through the pipeline, from elementary school to high school to college and all the way up the corporate ladder.

In 2015, just 22 percent of all the students who took the AP Computer Science exam were female. The problem persists through college, where young women tend to drop out of technology-related majors. Reynolds felt compelled to make her documentary after her own daughter dropped out of her college computer science program. Her daughter was one of only two girls in the class and felt that the guys knew more than she did. When it comes to careers, women hold just 26 percent of computing jobs and a mere 5 percent of company leadership positions in the technology industry.

The women who do make it through this pipeline and currently work in technology continue to fight biases every day. Tracy Chou is a software engineer at Pinterest who was interviewed for Reynolds's documentary. She's often told she doesn't look like a software engineer because she's a young woman. Biases and misconceptions lead to a work environment that is often uncomfortable and stifling for women. Many regularly feel isolated or excluded at work.

A female programmer often experiences the same kind of thing Kimberly Bryant did in her first engineering class; she's the only one in a room full of male colleagues, and she has to prove her right to be there. Her colleagues may even go so far as to make disparaging or sexist comments. Ashe Dryden has been a programmer for more than a decade. She says, "I've been harassed, I've had people make suggestive comments to me, I've had people basically dismiss my expertise … A lot of times that makes me want to leave."[6] If Dryden left the field, she'd unfortunately be among the majority. According to research from Harvard Business School, 56 percent of women working in technology leave by mid-career. That's twice the rate for men in the same field.

Facing Even Greater Obstacles

Being a girl who's interested in science and technology is hard enough. When that girl happens to be black, Latina, or American Indian, the path to success in a STEM field becomes even more riddled with obstacles. In 2015, just 13 percent of students taking the AP Computer Science exams were African American or Latino, of either gender. Though African American and Latino people make up 29 percent of the general workforce in the United States, just 15 percent of the computing workforce are African or Latino. Of that 15 percent, just 3 percent are African American women and 1 percent are Latina women.

A girl who isn't white has to deal with the same societal pressures as all other girls and overcome the myth of math and science as "guy things." Secondly, she must face a whole additional set of biases and challenges related to her racial background. African American people in the United States have historically been oppressed, and they still face discrimination despite laws to try to prevent unfair treatment. Part of the historical oppression has been an expectation that African Americans pursue careers deemed appropriate by the white majority, such as being teachers or farmers. Kimberly Bryant points out that the traditional image of success in African American culture has been to become a lawyer, doctor, or educator. "For African Americans from the US," she says, "engineering has not traditionally been a path that we've been known to push our kids into."[7] Plus, nowadays, kids from the African American communities she works with tend to aspire to be famous singers or sports stars.

While there's nothing wrong with any of those professions, it's troubling to Bryant and others that science and engineering often aren't even considered as options for young people of color. One important issue is that role models are few and far between. In music and sports, famous people of color abound, so it's easy for kids to see themselves in those roles. In technology, when a woman makes it to the top, she is usually white, such as Sheryl Sandberg, COO at Facebook. If there are no black, female superstars in technology, it's hard for little girls of color to see themselves in that role.

In addition, many of the communities of color that Bryant's organization targets are also low-income neighborhoods. Black Girls Code purposefully reaches out to these places since the kids there face yet another set of challenges related to their socioeconomic status. If being female and black weren't enough, poverty adds another huge hurdle onto these kids' paths toward a successful future. Most obviously, poverty makes it very difficult to access the tools needed to learn coding. It also increases kids' exposure to crime, drugs, hunger, violence, and other serious problems.

Learning to code offers a way out of that world. McKeever E. Conwell teaches at the nonprofit

Sheryl Sandberg, COO of Facebook, regularly speaks out about empowering women to achieve their goals, but young women of color may not feel that her message is meant for them.

organization Code Fever, which targets low-income communities in Miami, Florida. "I'm from Baltimore, the inner city. I did a lot of things an inner-city kid does," he said in a documentary produced by Black Girls Code. "Technology saved my life because it gave me something I thought was cool, I thought was interesting. It gave me something I could do after high school."[8] High-paying computer science jobs can transform the lives of girls and other children who grew up in poverty.

Planting the Seeds

Societal biases surrounding gender and race, a lack of role models, and a lack of access to computers, robots, and other essential tools all make it difficult for girls of color to see themselves as scientists or engineers. They often don't even realize that a career in technology is an option that exists. According to Bryant, when she started her pilot program in 2011, "most of the girls did not know what computer science was. They did not know what computer programming was. They had no clue."[9] It's not that they weren't interested in technology—they hadn't had a chance to find out if it's something that would interest them. Silicon Valley was right in their backyard, but it may as well have been another country.

Black Girls Code workshops transform girls' image of what coding is, and how difficult it is to do. Without any exposure to coding, robotics, and science in general, logically kids won't develop an interest in these fields.

Thinking about the program, Aliana Tejeda, a seventeen-year-old from New Jersey, said:[10]

> *Before I didn't believe I was even able to pursue such a career, however attending Black Girls Code helped me realize that coding isn't just for a select few, but for everyone, and that all I need to do is put my mind where my heart is and the rest comes easy.*[10]

At the end of any Black Girls Code class, all the girls have created something of their own using technology.

Kimberly Bryant hopes that the girls who go through her programs will continue to code and learn about science and technology on their own, but she knows that not all of them will. Some will follow other passions. All she wants to do is plant the seeds and give girls a way to picture possibilities for themselves that may not have been readily apparent. They won't all go on to become software engineers or found their own technology companies, but at least they know that the opportunity is out there. Some will become programmers or CEOs. Others will be astronauts, medical researchers, roboticists, or science educators. Logan, a Black Girls Code participant, says, "I learned from Ms. Kimberly Bryant that I can do whatever it is that I want to do because I am a black girl who rocks!!!"[11]

Thanks to Kimberly Bryant and her team of volunteers, kids who go through the Black Girls Code

Kimberly Bryant speaks at the 2016 opening of a new Black Girls Code space located at Google's offices in New York City.

program now see coding as an exciting pastime and a possible future career. Many of them will persevere, despite the myriad biases and stereotypes clouding their paths. The kicker is that the technology field really needs these kids. It needs as much talent as it can get.

Paradoxically, as girls and young people of color lose interest in science and math or grow up oblivious to a technology career as an option, the field of technology is expanding by leaps and bounds. Companies are scrambling to find enough people with the right skills to fill software-engineering jobs and other technical roles. The US Department of Labor predicts that there will be approximately 1.2 million computing-related job openings by 2022. And these will be some of the highest-paid positions in the workforce. The median wage for a software developer is just over $100,000, according to the US Bureau of Labor Statistics. Yet at the current graduation rate, US computing graduates will be able to fill just 39 percent of those 1.2 million jobs. Kimberly Bryant would argue that the people the tech industry needs are right there in one of her workshops. They are the girls and young people of color who otherwise wouldn't know how much they love coding. Society's biases and stereotypes are causing the technology industry to lose out on a huge pool of talent.

This issue is so important that the US government has recognized and responded with a program called Computer Science for All. Barack Obama launched the initiative in January 2016 with the goal of giving every student access to the computer science and math classes that they will need to be ready for their careers. In addition to getting more schools to offer computer science programs, the initiative aims to address the lack of diversity that prompted Bryant to start Black Girls Code. In a statement, the White House wrote, "Tech careers are exciting, fun, high-impact, and collaborative as well as being critical for our economy. We want all Americans to have the opportunity to be part of these teams."[12]

From Discrimination to Diversity

Teaching girls and kids from underrepresented communities to love coding isn't going to be enough. The technology industry itself has to change as well to become more open and welcoming. Just as it's hard for a young black woman to see herself in a technology position when she has no role models who've experienced success in that career, it can be equally difficult for a hiring manager to see that young woman as someone who is a good fit for the position.

Even if the hiring manager has the best intentions to hire without discrimination based on race or gender, implicit biases still make a difference. In a 2012 study, Yale researchers sent applications for a lab manager position out to six different colleges and universities. The applications were all identical, except for the fact that some had a male name on them and others a female name. The applications with a male name were rated as more competent and hirable, and were offered a higher starting salary. People from minority groups face similar biases. A 2016 study sent out 1,600 fake résumés, all based off of real ones. Some of these résumés had been left alone, while others had been edited to change any information that might suggest that the person's race was anything other than white. The African American job seekers received callbacks for 10 percent of their original résumés, but 25.5 percent of their "whitened" résumés.

Clearly, discrimination remains a problem for both women and minorities in the workforce.

Kimberly Bryant argues that this discrimination is not just a problem for the people who are marginalized and left out of the tech industry; it's also a problem for the industry itself. Research backs up this assessment. A 2014 MIT study found that gender diversity was correlated with higher productivity in the workplace. Other forms of diversity matter, too. In a 2015 report, McKinsey, a management consulting firm, found that companies with high gender, racial, or ethnic diversity were more likely to have higher profits than companies with low diversity. Conversely, companies with low diversity were also more likely to perform worse than the rest of the pack.

To Bryant, it's clear why companies should focus on diversity. When girls and women drop out of the pipeline and abandon what could have been promising careers in technology, their contributions are lost. Bryant points out that women make up half of the world's population. "By limiting women in technology, we are limiting ourselves to only half of the world's solutions," she says.[13] While lifting up women in general is important to Bryant, she is frustrated that many companies' diversity programs mainly benefit white women. She says, "If a company is really committed to diversity, that means everything. That means gender diversity, that means sexual orientation … that means race, ethnicity."[14] Age diversity is yet another aspect of the problem.

Studies have shown that very diverse companies tend to earn higher profits than companies with low diversity.

If a company wants to be successful, Bryant says, its workforce must reflect the customers it wants to serve. In order to create products that will resonate with women, people of color, or other marginalized communities, these people must be present during the design and development process. If a company wants its software to be on everyone's devices, it needs employees who actually represent "everyone." It's not enough for executives to shrug their shoulders and say that there aren't enough applicants from diverse backgrounds. It's their responsibility, Bryant argues, to go out and find the people they need to make the best products.

Though Hispanic people or people of African descent are currently minority groups in the United States, the populations of both of these groups are growing. As of 2014, over half of the children under five years old living in the United States were from minority groups. It's essential that these kids learn about technology and coding as they grow up. Technical skills will open the doors to high-salary jobs for these children once they grow up, and society as a whole will benefit from having additional innovators working in technology. Teaching girls and kids from minority groups to code is a win-win situation. Furthermore, Bryant argues that true diversity goes beyond the borders of the country you live in. The audience for technology is worldwide, and creators of technology could come from any and all cultures. A focus on diversity gives a company access to innovative ideas and perspectives that could only come from the unique life experiences of people from many different backgrounds.

Though diversity is still a big problem in the technology industry, it's an issue that is garnering more and more support. When Bryant started Black Girls Code, it was relatively rare for her to hear people talking about a diversity problem. Now, these issues are front and center, where they should be. "Everywhere you look there is a conversation about the role of gender and diversity in tech. It's not something that is done undercover," says Bryant.[15] Big corporations such as Google, Twitter,

Apple, and Facebook have released the numbers of women and people of color working at their companies.

While all of these tech giants' employee populations are still overwhelmingly white and male, the numbers of women, people of color, and other minority groups are slowly increasing. All of these companies have committed resources to increasing diversity or even to funding coding education. In fact, the Black Girls Code chapter in New York is located within Google's offices and is sponsored by the company. With so many people, corporations, and organizations working to create change, Kimberly Bryant says, it's bound to happen.

The Learn to Code Movement

Around the same time Kimberly Bryant founded Black Girls Code, dozens of other similar organizations were also taking root. Through the 2010s, the "Learn to Code" movement exploded. All of these organizations were responding to similar problems: a lack of coding and computer science curriculum in schools, a lack of graduates with the skills needed for technical careers, and a lack of diversity in science and technology. Each organization has a slightly different focus area. Code.org, one of the largest organizations, aims to increase awareness and bring computer science education to every student in every school. In its annual "Hour of Code" campaign, people around the world organize events for participants ages 4 to 104 to try coding. Coder Dojo organizes programming clubs for young people. Code academy offers free online courses in coding.

Other organizations target specific communities. Code Now runs free computer science workshops for students from underrepresented backgrounds. Girls Who Code focuses on the gender gap with clubs and immersion programs for girls. And the Hidden Genius Project offers computer science and tech training for African American boys. However, Black Girls Code remains the only coding organization to focus specifically on girls of color. To Kimberly Bryant, that intersection of race and gender is significant enough to merit a special program.

CHAPTER SIX

Reaching a Million Girls

K imberly Bryant has a lofty goal for Black Girls Code: she aims to reach one million girls by 2040. As of 2016, she had reached almost eight thousand. That's an incredible achievement considering that she started with a class of just twelve girls five years earlier in 2011. Numerous institutions, including the White House and Bryant's role model Oprah Winfrey, have recognized her accomplishments. Though Bryant spends a lot of time traveling and speaking about diversity, she remains involved in the day-to-day operations of Black Girls Code. She focuses mainly on keeping the

Kimberly Bryant accepts the Include Diversity Award at TechCrunch's 2016 ceremony honoring important figures in technology.

curriculum relevant, adding new chapters and programs, and getting funding for the organization's activities.

A Champion of Change

Since Kimberly Bryant founded Black Girls Code, she's received numerous awards and other honors for her work. In 2012, she was a local winner of the Jefferson Award for Public Service for her work in the San Francisco Bay Area. The Jefferson Awards Foundation is dedicated to recognizing outstanding public service and inspiring more people to get involved in their communities. The White House honored Bryant in 2013 as a Champion of Change for Tech Inclusion. During a panel discussion with ten other winners of the honor, Bryant talked about being able to see the impoverished neighborhood of Bayview-Hunters Point from the back door of the biotech company where she worked in Silicon Valley. She saw herself in the kids living there, since she had grown up in the inner city of Memphis. She said, "We cannot lose another generation. We can't afford it as a community; we can't afford it as a nation to have a generation left behind without access to technology tools."[1]

Kimberly Bryant has also shown up on numerous lists recognizing important or influential people. In 2013, she was on *Business Insider*'s list of the 25 Most Influential African Americans in Technology as well as the Root 100 and the Ebony Power 100, both lists that recognize influential African Americans in business, science, politics, technology, sports, and more. In 2014, she made it onto the Good 100, a list that celebrates individuals at the cutting edge of creative impact, the Government Technology Top 25 Doers, Dreamers, and Drivers, the Forty Over 40 list of middle-aged women who are making an impact, the Marie Claire list of 20 Women Changing the World, and the CNN 10 Visionary Women list.

That same year, she received a Women Who Rule Award in Technology from *Politico*, Google, and the Tory Burch Foundation, as well as a Smithsonian American Ingenuity Award in Social Progress. In a video for the Smithsonian award, Bryant said:

This is not just a path that I started because it's the right thing to do. These girls are me, thirty, forty years ago. To be able to touch these girls like my daughter and other daughters gives me a sense of accomplishment that I've never gotten with anything else before.[2]

In 2014, Kimberly Bryant also got her wish to meet her role model, Oprah Winfrey, in real life. During a multi-city tour called "The Life You Want Weekend," Winfrey awarded Bryant with the Toyota Standing O-vation Award for her work. Bryant had no idea she was going to receive the award and was overwhelmed with emotion when she got up on stage to receive it.

Over the past several years, Bryant has continued to receive awards. TechCrunch, a website covering technology news, hosts an annual award ceremony called the Crunchies, described as the Oscars of start-ups and technology. Kimberly Bryant won the inaugural Include Diversity Award during the 2016 Crunchies. During her acceptance speech, she said, "It's an honor to receive the very first TechCrunch Include award ... The work we do is creating opportunities so in a few years there won't be a need for this award."[3] Bryant also serves on the board of several organizations, including the National Champions Board for the National Girls Collaborative Project and the National Board of the National Center for Women and Information Technology K-12 Alliance.

From Wearable Devices to Virtual Reality

Kimberly Bryant doesn't let her numerous awards distract her from her goals. If anything, all this recognition inspires her to work even harder. To ensure that her organization continues to grow, Kimberly Bryant must keep up with changes in the fast-paced technology field. New coding languages, operating systems, software, and hardware continually change the landscape for people working in technology. Educators must update their teaching materials to make sure that their students enter the workforce with relevant skills. In addition to being able to create mobile applications, websites, and robots, the next generation of coders must also understand cutting-edge technology such as the **internet of things** and **virtual reality**. The internet of things (IoT) is a network in which sensors on physical devices collect information and exchange it with applications or other devices through the internet. A virtual-reality (VR) device is typically worn over the eyes and allows a user to experience a virtual world as if it is the real world.

Black Girls Code has already started introducing the internet of things in its workshops, Bryant says. On December 10, 2016, the New York chapter of Black Girls Code held a one-day event titled: "We CREATE! A Parent-Daughter Circuits and IoT Workshop." The IoT concept is easy for Black Girls Code students to grasp since they've grown up in a world with devices such as the Fitbit, a wearable fitness tracker, and the Apple Watch, a watch-sized version of an iPhone. In some of these new workshops, Bryant says, "the girls have been creating multi-tiered applications where a mobile app attaches to a wearable device."[4] Her students are interested in all aspects of this technology, including the app, the interface between the device and the app, and the device itself. This kind of workshop links the digital world to the physical world, Bryant says, which can help make technology even more relevant to the kids.

Bryant is also interested in eventually introducing workshops in virtual reality or its cousin, augmented reality. The hit game *Pokémon Go* is an example of augmented reality. The mobile game shows the real world as if the player is looking through a camera, but digital creatures called Pokémon show up on the screen, too, as if they are out there in the real world. The player has to go to real places in order to capture and collect the creatures. Virtual-reality headsets such as the Oculus Rift, HTC Vive, and PlayStation VR were all released to the public for the first time in 2016 and are mainly used to play video games. "This is the generation of seeing VR come to life,"[5] Bryant says. In the future, her students will be developing software for these new technologies as well as others that haven't even been invented yet.

To Europe and Beyond

Developing new curriculum is important, but won't directly help Bryant achieve her goal of reaching a million girls. To do that, she must expand her organization. Dozens of cities in the United States and around the world have expressed interest in hosting a chapter of Black Girls Code. But it takes time to obtain funding for a new chapter and to find the local coordinators and volunteers necessary to run events there. Bryant says that her greatest challenge right now is growing quickly enough to meet demand.

She's especially interested in expanding into the Midwest, Europe, and Canada. Her organization began on the West Coast in California and has since expanded to multiple cities on the East Coast, but the group still isn't reaching very many students in the middle of the country. Bryant would especially love to open another chapter in Texas, as well as ones in Minneapolis and Kansas City. Though Black Girls Code works mostly with

Open Source Technology

It's not always easy for students to gain access to the development tools necessary to create applications for new devices. The tools may cost money to use, or the companies producing the devices may only grant access to developers that they approve. For example, the company Apple developed a programming language called Swift for use with its devices. It wasn't until 2015 that this language became open source, or freely available, to all developers. Bryant is a big fan of open-source technology because it makes coding accessible to more students. She points out that companies can nurture new talent for their organizations through open-source tools. Since 2015, it's been much easier for her group to teach development for Apple devices. She hopes that platforms used for developing virtual-reality applications will become open source in the near future.

girls of color living in America, Bryant would also love to expand her group's international reach. Black Girls Code already has a chapter in Johannesburg, South Africa. In the next few years, they may open more chapters in Africa, as well as new ones in Europe and Canada. London has expressed interest, as have several African countries, including Kenya, Ghana, and Liberia. "We think of ourselves as a global movement," Bryant says.[6]

In addition to geographic expansion, the organization has also experimented with outreach to different target audiences. To help get more girls from Hispanic communities involved, the group teamed up with Latino Startup Alliance in 2014 to launch La TechLa, a crowdfunded program that supported bilingual workshops for girls in ten cities across the United States as well as in Puerto Rico and Mexico. Since then, Black Girls Code and Latino Startup Alliance have continued to work together to bring Black Girls Code workshops to girls who speak Spanish as their native language.

Black Girls Code has also offered workshops for parents and their daughters to attend together. In addition, boys have been invited to some workshops. Though the group will always focus primarily on girls, Bryant recognizes that sometimes it makes sense to include both. As early as 2012, the group hosted a one-day game development class for both boys and girls in San Francisco. Many of the parents and grandparents stuck around for the workshop, too. At the end of the class, one of the boys said, "So is this what a software engineer does? Then I'm interested in being an engineer."[7] Bryant recognizes how important it is to motivate boys of color along with their sisters. Plus, parents are always asking for ways to get their sons involved. Bryant has discussed the possibility of launching a partner organization called Black Boys Code.

Changing the Face of Technology

The boy who was interested in being an engineer after attending one workshop is just one example of the many lives Bryant's work has affected. The organization has heaps of anecdotal evidence that its programs have succeeded in sending students on a trajectory toward a career in technology. Bryant has heard from parents that girls who have attended her programs have started to perform better in math classes at school. Some former students are now pursuing degrees in computer science at college and have pointed to Black Girls Code as the primary influence for their decision.

To back up these stories and truly measure the success of the program, Bryant's organization will need to collect objective data. First of all, she wants to see whether girls from her program are really performing better in math and science classes than their peers who haven't attended any workshops. To do this, she will have to compare math and science test scores from each group. "If there is a direct correlation and we can prove that, then I think that supports the argument that coding really helps kids in other areas of school, in other areas of life," she says. "And it makes computer science a beneficial skill for all students to learn, regardless of whether they want to be a software engineer or not."[8]

In addition, Bryant hopes to follow the girls and track their progress after they leave the program. She points to two key measuring blocks that she plans to use. First of all, she wants to count how many Black Girls Code students end up taking the AP Computer Science exam. Then, she also wants to count how many go on to enroll in a college, university, or technical degree program in a STEM field. To collect all of this information, her group has applied for research grants. Once girls in the program go off to college, Bryant hopes that they'll remain involved in Black Girls Code. She plans to build an internship program to help older or more advanced students return to events as mentors.

The real measure of success for Kimberly Bryant, though, will come when the girls from her program begin changing the world through their careers. Her students are already imagining the impact that they will have. Black Girls Code partnered with 20th Century Fox, producer of the January 2017 film *Hidden Figures,* which is about Katherine Johnson and two other African American women who played important roles at NASA during the space race of the 1950s and 1960s. To celebrate the film, Black Girls Code students created a website called Future Katherine Johnsons. On the website, fourteen girls each coded their own page to talk about how Katherine Johnson inspired them and what they hope to do with their futures. Skylar, an eleven-year-old, said, "She has inspired me to become a better student so that one day I can be the scientist controlling the rover when it lands on Mars. My dream is that the rover I control will find intelligent extraterrestrial life."9 And Charmienne, a thirteen-year-old, said, "I hope to show other girls my age that they can do amazing things to have an impact for humanity and the planet through science by creating energy, conserving resources and curing

Black Girls Code participants attend a special screening of the 2017 movie *Hidden Figures,* which profiles African American women who contributed to NASA's space program.

diseases."10 Many girls in the program have similar visions for their futures. One girl wants to design math games, and another wants to build a video game using her own drawings. Another wants to go into science in order to help people around the world who are sick.

These girls envision themselves as engineers, programmers, scientists, astronauts, doctors, and more. They see themselves improving people's lives, helping others, and making the world a better place. Thanks to Bryant's work, it's now very likely that the founder of the next Google or Facebook will be a woman of color. The Black Girls Code revolution is changing the face of technology.

1968

Dr. Martin Luther King Jr. is fatally shot in Kimberly Bryant's home city of Memphis, Tennessee.

2010

Kimberly Bryant leaves her corporate job with the goal of founding a start-up biotechnology company.

1998

Kimberly Bryant starts working in the biomedical industry for Merck & Co., then moves on to a job at Pfizer, Inc.

Kimberly Bryant is born.

1967

Kimberly Bryant moves to San Francisco for a job at the biomedical company Genentech, Inc.

2006

Kimberly Bryant graduates from Vanderbilt University with a degree in electrical engineering and computer science.

1989

2014

Oprah Winfrey awards Kimberly Bryant with a Standing O-vation on her "Life You Want Weekend" tour.

2012

Black Girls Code opens local chapters in several other US cities as well as one international chapter in Johannesburg, South Africa.

Kimberly Bryant founds Black Girls Code, an organization devoted to getting girls of color interested in coding and careers in technology. The group holds its first workshop in the community of Bayview-Hunters Point in San Francisco, California.

A Black Girls Code workshop appears in a cameo on the Fox TV show *Empire*.

2016

The White House honors Kimberly Bryant as a Champion of Change for Tech Inclusion.

2011

2013

SOURCE NOTES

Chapter 1

1. Kimberly Bryant, "Black Girls Code," TEDxKC, YouTube video, October 5, 2013, https://www.youtube.com/watch?v=TJ-m47CxAI0.

2. Martin Luther King Jr., "I Have a Dream," speech delivered August 28, 1963, American Rhetoric, Accessed December 17, 2016, http://www.americanrhetoric.com/speeches/mlkihaveadream.htm.

3. Bryant, "Black Girls Code" TEDxKC video.

4. Ibid.

5. Tishin Donkersley, "Black Girls Code Founder Kimberly Bryant Helping Little Girls Change the World—Interview," AZ Tech Beat, June 11, 2015, http://aztechbeat.com/2015/06/black-girls-code-founder-kimberly-bryant-helping-little-girls-change-the-world-interview.

6. Kimberly Bryant, "Planting Seeds of Innovation," TEDx St. Louis, YouTube video, December 23, 2013, https://www.youtube.com/watch?v=5izVLqwdVqs.

7. Gail Collins, *When Everything Changed: The Amazing Journey of American Women from 1960 to the Present* (New York: Little, Brown and Company, 2009), Accessed December 17, 2009, http://www.npr.org/2009/10/14/113764557/author-economic-changes-opened-doors-for-women.

8. Evelyn Boyd Granville, "My Life as a Mathematician," Agnes Scott College, Accessed December 17, 2016, https://www.agnesscott.edu/lriddle/women/granvill.htm.

9. Sal Khan, "Sal Khan with Black Girls Code's Kimberly Bryant," INFORUM at the Commonwealth Club, YouTube video, April 8, 2015, https://www.youtube.com/watch?v=Yeb8TuuTdwg.

10. Kimberly Bryant, "Kimberly Bryant Speaks at Female Founders Conference 2015," Y Combinator, YouTube video, February 23, 2015, https://www.youtube.com/watch?v=qeeRsWofAv0.

11. Ibid.

Chapter 2

1. Khan, "Sal Khan with Black Girls Code's Kimberly Bryant" video.

2. Ibid.

3. Ibid.

4. Ibid.

5. Ibid.

6. Amy Rose Spiegel, "Black Girls Code Founder Kimberly Bryant Talks Her Favorite Apps, Diversity in the Tech World, and More," Complex, October 24, 2016, http://www.complex.com/life/2016/10/black-girls-code-kimberly-bryant-interview.

7. Lisa A. Dubois, "Kimberly Bryant, BE'89, Is Changing the Face of High-Tech with Black Girls Code," *Vanderbilt Magazine*, September 26, 2014, https://news.vanderbilt.edu/vanderbiltmagazine/kimberly-bryant-is-changing-the-face-of-high-tech-with-black-girls-code.

8. Spiegel, "Black Girls Code Founder Kimberly Bryant Talks Her Favorite Apps, Diversity in the Tech World, and More."

9. Donkersley, "Black Girls Code Founder Kimberly Bryant Helping Little Girls Change the World—Interview."

10. Greg Greenlee, "#BITTechTalk with Guest Kimberly Bryant," Blacks in Technology podcast, Episode 23, November 17, 2011, https://www.blacksintechnology.net/bittechtalk-episode-23-with-guest-kimberly-bryant.

11. Leonie Wedderburn, "Recommendation," LinkedIn, February 12, 2009, https://www.linkedin.com/in/leonie-a-wedderburn-65628010.

12. Sandor Schoichet, "Recommendation," LinkedIn, September 17, 2010, https://www.linkedin.com/in/sschoichet.

13. Spiegel, "Black Girls Code Founder Kimberly Bryant Talks Her Favorite Apps, Diversity in the Tech World, and More."

14. Amanda L'Esperance, "Recommendation," LinkedIn, January 11, 2011, https://www.linkedin.com/in/kimberlybryant.

Chapter 3

1. Bryant, "Black Girls Code" TEDxKC video.

2. Dubois, "Kimberly Bryant, BE'89, Is Changing the Face of High-Tech with Black Girls Code."

3. Vanity Fair Studios with IBM, "Saluting a New Guard of STEM Stars, Part 2," *Vanity Fair*, December 2016, http://www.vanityfair.com/news/2016/12/saluting-a-new-guard-of-stem-stars-part-2.

4. Angela Dawson, "Maker Mom Kimberly Bryant Builds Futures with Black Girls Code." Not Impossible Now, March 23, 2015, http://www.notimpossiblenow.com/lives/kimberly-bryant.

5. Khan, "Sal Khan with Black Girls Code's Kimberly Bryant" video.

6. Kai Morton, "My Techie Summer," Black Girls Code, August 5, 2011, http://www.blackgirlscode.com/blog/archives/08-2011.

7. Khan, "Sal Khan with Black Girls Code's Kimberly Bryant" video.

8. Spiegel, "Black Girls Code Founder Kimberly Bryant Talks Her Favorite Apps, Diversity in the Tech World, and More."

9. CNN, "The CNN 10 Visionary Women," CNN, March 2014, Accessed December 19, 2016, http://www.cnn.com/interactive/2014/03/living/cnn10-visionary-women.

10. Spiegel, "Black Girls Code Founder Kimberly Bryant Talks Her Favorite Apps, Diversity in the Tech World, and More."

11. Khan, "Sal Khan with Black Girls Code's Kimberly Bryant" video.

12. Lyndsey Gilpin, "Black Girls Code Founder Kimberly Bryant: Engineer. Entrepreneur. Mother." TechRepublic, April 7, 2014, http://www.techrepublic.com/article/black-girls-code-founder-kimberly-bryant-engineer-entrepreneur-mother.

13. Kimberly Bryant, "In Search of a Black Mark Zuckerberg: Why I Founded Black Girls Code," Black Girls Code, April 10, 2011, http://www.blackgirlscode.com/blog/archives/04-2011.

14. Kimberly Bryant, "In the Beginning—BlackGirlsCODE Summer of Code," Black Girls Code, June 14, 2012, http://www.blackgirlscode.com/blog/in-the-beginning-blackgirlscode-summer-of-code.

15. Khan, "Sal Khan with Black Girls Code's Kimberly Bryant" video.

16. Nailah. "KidsRuby and Me!" Black Girls Code, October 3, 2011, http://www.blackgirlscode.com/blog/kidsruby-and-me.

17. Kai Morton, "A Good Day to Learn KidsRuby!" Black Girls Code, September 23, 2011, http://www.blackgirlscode.com/blog/archives/09-2011.

18. Dawson, "Maker Mom Kimberly Bryant Builds Futures With Black Girls Code."

19. Gilpin, "Black Girls Code founder Kimberly Bryant: Engineer. Entrepreneur. Mother."

20. Donkersley, "Black Girls Code Founder Kimberly Bryant Helping Little Girls Change the World—Interview."

Chapter 4

1. Kimberly Bryant, "Behind the Click: Securing the Future for Girls of Color as the Tech Leaders and Creators of Tomorrow," School of Engineering, Vanderbilt University, February 24, 2014, http://engineering.vanderbilt.edu/news/2014/behind-the-click-securing-the-future-for-girls-of-color-as-the-tech-leaders-and-creators-of-tomorrow,

2. OneDublin.org. "Black Girls Code Founder Kimberly Bryant on Inspiring Students to Pursue STEM," OneDublin.org, January 20, 2014, https://onedublin.org/2014/01/20/black-girls-code-founder-kimberly-bryant-on-inspiring-students-to-pursue-stem.

3. Georgia Tech, "120+ Young Women Participate in Black Girls Code Robot Expo." Georgia Tech, October 26, 2016, http://www.scs.gatech.edu/news/583177/120-young-women-participate-black-girls-code-robot-expo.

4. Eric Westervelt, "'Disrupting' Tech's Diversity Problem with a Code Camp for Girls of Color." NPR, August 17, 2015, http://www.npr.org/sections/ed/2015/08/17/432278262/hacking-tech-s-diversity-problem-black-girls-code.

5. Spiegel, "Black Girls Code Founder Kimberly Bryant Talks Her Favorite Apps, Diversity in the Tech World, and More."

6. John Kennedy, "Kimberly Bryant: 'We Want to Introduce 1m Girls to Coding by 2040' (Video)," *Silicon Republic*, June

19, 2015, https://www.siliconrepublic.com/people/we-want-to-introduce-1m-girls-to-coding-by-2040-kimberly-bryant-tells-inspirefest.

7. Joyce Philippe, "'Black Girls Code' Aims to Break Racial and Gender Barriers in STEM," *Joyce Meets World*, April 1, 2014, http://www.joycemeetsworld.com/index.php/2014/04.

8. Bryant, "Behind the Click."

9. Catherine D'Ignazio, "Kimberly Bryant and Black Girls Code," MIT Media Lab, November 18, 2013, http://diversity.media.mit.edu/2013/11/18/271.

10. Vanity Fair Studios with IBM, "Saluting a New Guard of STEM Stars, Part 2."

11. Shanice Malakai Johnson, "Black Girls Code Ep #1: The Revolution Will Be Mobilized," Black Girls Code, YouTube video, October 14, 2013, https://www.youtube.com/watch?v=AQJU6ehn6-s&feature=youtu.be.

12. Ibid.

13. Scott Hanselman, "Improving Diversity in Technology with Kimberly Bryant from BlackGirlsCode.com," Hanselminutes podcast, Show 303, January 26, 2012, http://hanselminutes.com/303/improving-diversity-in-technology-with-kimberly-bryant-from-blackgirlscodecom.

14. Thornton May, "Women and the Future of IT," *Computer World*, January 7, 2015, http://www.computerworld.com/article/2866426/women-and-the-future-of-it.html.

15. Mary K. Pratt, "Black Girls Code Founder Looks to Expand Skills Outreach, Challenges CIOs to Help the Cause," *Computer World*, February 11, 2015, http://www.computerworld.com/article/2877211/black-girls-code-founder-looks-to-expand-skills-outreach-challenges-cios-to-help-the-cause.html.

16. Bryant, "Behind the Click."

17. Kennedy, "Kimberly Bryant: 'We Want to Introduce 1m Girls to Coding by 2040' (Video)."

18. Colm Gorey, "Black Girls Code Hits the Big Time with *Empire* Cameo." *Silicon Republic*, October 6, 2016, https://www.siliconrepublic.com/life/black-girls-code-empire-cameo.

19. Spur, "2016 Silver SPUR Awards: Kimberly Bryant," Spur, Vimeo video, November 17, 2016, https://vimeo.com/192844021.

Chapter 5

1. Pratt, "Black Girls Code Founder Looks to Expand Skills Outreach, Challenges CIOs to Help the Cause."

2. Bryant, "Black Girls Code" TEDxKC video.

3. Kimberly Bryant, "Inspirefest—Code: Debugging the Gender Gap—Kimberly Bryant, Founder, Black Girls Code," Silicon Republic, YouTube video, June 19, 2015, https://www.youtube.com/watch?v=gfBlg4SaCSE.

4. Adobe, "Adobe's Youth Coding Initiative: Black Girls Code," Adobe, YouTube video, November 17, 2015, https://www.youtube.com/watch?v=nyEr2xHtOVU.

5. Marco della Cava, "Why Women Won't Code Is Topic of New Documentary," *USA Today*, March 30, 2015, http://www.usatoday.com/story/tech/2015/03/30/women-coding-code-debugging-the-gender-gap-premiers-at-tribeca-film-festival/70693424.

6. Claire Cain Miller, "Technology's Man Problem," *New York Times*, April 5, 2014, https://www.nytimes.com/2014/04/06/technology/technologys-man-problem.html?_r=0.

7. Hanselman, "Improving Diversity in Technology with Kimberly Bryant from BlackGirlsCode.com" podcast.

8. Shanice Malakai Johnson, "Black Girls Code Series Ep #2: Miami," Black Girls Code, YouTube video, February 28, 2014, https://www.youtube.com/watch?v=acl_orsqXVg.

9. Hanselman, "Improving Diversity in Technology with Kimberly Bryant from BlackGirlsCode.com" podcast.

10. Debra Rosenberg, "Could This Be the Answer to the Tech World's Diversity Problem?" *Smithsonian*, November 2014, http://www.smithsonianmag.com/ innovation/answer-tech-worlds-diversity-problem-180953046/#qCpDq1gLZ8ARbeYt.99.

11. Johnson, "Black Girls Code Series Ep #2: Miami" video.

12. Megan Smith, "Computer Science for All," White House, January 30, 2016, https://www.whitehouse.gov/ blog/2016/01/30/computer-science-all.

13. John Kennedy, "The Week Ahead: A New Tipping Point for the Tech Industry," *Silicon Republic*, June 22, 2015, https:// www.siliconrepublic.com/business/the-week-ahead-a-new-tipping-point-for-the-tech-industry.

14. Megan Rose Dickey, "Black Girls Code Founder Kimberly Bryant on Racism and Implicit Bias," TechCrunch, February 1, 2016, https://techcrunch.com/2016/02/01/black-girls-code-founder-kimberly-bryant-on-racism-and-implicit-bias.

15. Angela Tafoya, "This Woman Could Change Everything You Believe About Tech: Superwoman Kimberly Bryant," *Refinery29*, September 8, 2014, http://www.refinery29.com/ kimberly-bryant.

Chapter 6

1. Todd Park, "Honoring Tech Inclusion Champions of Change at the White House," White House, August 8, 2013, https://www.whitehouse.gov/blog/2013/08/08/honoring-tech-inclusion-champions-change-white-house.

2. "Smithsonian Ingenuity Awards 2014: Kimberly Bryant." *Smithsonian*, Accessed January 2, 2017, http://www.smithsonianmag.com/videos/category/innovation/smithsonian-ingenuity-awards-2014-kimberly/#ooid=0zbjQ1cTpeFXqrFbo4FkVep3CQQwJk4s.

3. "Kimberly Bryant Wins the Include Diversity Award at the 9th Annual Crunchies." TechCrunch, February 9, 2016, https://techcrunch.com/video/kimberly-bryant-wins-the-include-diversity-award-at-the-9th-annual-crunchies/519483338.

4. Spiegel, "Black Girls Code Founder Kimberly Bryant Talks Her Favorite Apps, Diversity in the Tech World, and More."

5. Ibid.

6. Pratt, "Black Girls Code Founder Looks to Expand Skills Outreach, Challenges CIOs to Help the Cause."

7. "Our Summer of Code Begins!" Black Girls Code, June 17, 2012, http://www.blackgirlscode.com/blog/our-summer-of-code-begins.

8. Tony Wan, "Where Diversity, Inclusion and Education Meet: A Conversation with Black Girls Code Founder, Kimberly Bryant," EdSurge News, October 23, 2016, https://www.edsurge.com/news/2016-10-23-where-diversity-inclusion-and-education-meet-a-conversation-with-black-girls-code-founder-kimberly-bryant.

9. "Future Katherine Johnsons." Black Girls Code, Accessed January 2, 2017, http://www.futurekatherinejohnsons.com.

10. Ibid.

GLOSSARY

bias An unfair assumption about a thing, person, or group.

biotech Short for "biotechnology," a field involving the manipulation or genetic engineering of living organisms or cells for use in medications or other products.

computer science The study of computing, programming, and algorithms used in computer systems.

curriculum The lessons and teaching materials comprising an entire course of study.

discrimination Unjust treatment of a group of people based on an attribute such as race, age, or sex.

diversity The inclusion of many different types of people in a group.

electrical engineering A branch of engineering that deals with electricity and electronic technology.

entrepreneur A person who starts and runs a business.

internet of things (IoT) A network of sensors on physical objects that collect and exchange information with online computer programs.

nonprofit An organization that does not aim to make a profit but rather exists to advance a cause.

prejudice A preconceived idea that is not based on factual evidence.

self-efficacy A belief in one's ability to succeed.

software engineering A branch of engineering that deals with the design, development, and maintenance of computer programs.

STEM An acronym often used in education to refer to science, technology, engineering, and math.

stereotype A widely shared image or idea about a particular type of person or thing.

virtual reality (VR) An experience that seems like the real world but is actually a computerized simulation.

FURTHER INFORMATION

Books

Morrison, Heather S. *Inventors of Computer Technology*. Designing Engineering Solutions. New York: Cavendish Square, 2016.

Pettinella, Amy. *Sheryl Sandberg*. Leading Women. New York: Cavendish Square, 2014.

Ryckman, Tatiana. *Oprah Winfrey*. Leading Women. New York: Cavendish Square, 2017.

Websites

Black Girls Code
http://www.blackgirlscode.com

The official website of Kimberly Bryant's organization features information about events, a blog with photos and stories about the program, and links to the group's social media sites.

Blacks in Technology
https://www.blacksintechnology.net

This website features a series of podcasts and articles profiling people of color working in technology. The site aims to increase the visibility and participation of people of color in the industry.

Codeacademy
https://www.codecademy.com

This website offers free courses and other tools to help people learn how to write code.

Computer Science for All
https://www.whitehouse.gov/blog/2016/01/30/computer-science-all

In 2016, President Barack Obama launched an initiative to bring computer science education to all students.

Girls Who Code
https://girlswhocode.com

This nonprofit organization aims to close the gender gap in technology through clubs and summer immersion coding programs for girls.

National Center for Women and Information Technology
https://www.ncwit.org

The National Science Foundation founded this nonprofit organization in 2004 with the goal of increasing the number of women and girls in computing.

Videos

Hauser, Robin, director. *CODE: Debugging the Gender Gap.* **Finish Line Features, 2015.**
This documentary looks at reasons why there are so few women and minorities working in the technology industry and explores ways to address the problem.

Johnson, Shanice Malakai. *Black Girls Code.* **MalakaiCreative. com, 2013, https://www.youtube.com/user/BlackGirlsCode/ videos**
This series of three short documentaries profiles some of the teachers, volunteers, and students participating in Black Girls Code workshops.

BIBLIOGRAPHY

Bryant, Kimberly. "Behind the Click: Securing the Future for Girls of Color as the Tech Leaders and Creators of Tomorrow." School of Engineering, Vanderbilt University, February 24, 2014. http://engineering.vanderbilt.edu/news/2014/behind-the-click-securing-the-future-for-girls-of-color-as-the-tech-leaders-and-creators-of-tomorrow.

———. "Black Girls Code." TEDxKC, YouTube video, October 5, 2013. https://www.youtube.com/watch?v=TJ-m47CxAI0.

———. "Changing the Face of Technology—One Girl at a Time." *Huffington Post*, September 29, 2015. http://www.huffingtonpost.com/kimberly-bryant/changing-the-face-of-tech_b_8208306.html.

———. "In Search of a Black Mark Zuckerberg: Why I Founded Black Girls Code." Black Girls Code, April 10, 2011. http://www.blackgirlscode.com/blog/archives/04-2011.

———. "Planting Seeds of Innovation." TEDx St. Louis, YouTube video, December 23, 2013. https://www.youtube.com/watch?v=5izVLqwdVqs.

Dawson, Angela. "Maker Mom Kimberly Bryant Builds Futures with Black Girls Code." Not Impossible Now, March 23, 2015. http://www.notimpossiblenow.com/lives/kimberly-bryant.

Dickey, Megan Rose. "Black Girls Code Founder Kimberly Bryant on Racism and Implicit Bias." TechCrunch, February 1, 2016. https://techcrunch.com/2016/02/01/black-girls-code-founder-kimberly-bryant-on-racism-and-implicit-bias.

D'Ignazio, Catherine. "Kimberly Bryant and Black Girls Code." MIT Media Lab, November 18, 2013. http://diversity.media. mit.edu/2013/11/18/271.

Donkersley, Tishin. "Black Girls Code Founder Kimberly Bryant Helping Little Girls Change the World—Interview." AZ Tech Beat, June 11, 2015. http://aztechbeat.com/2015/06/ black-girls-code-founder-kimberly-bryant-helping-little-girls-change-the-world-interview.

Dubois, Lisa A. "Kimberly Bryant, BE'89, Is Changing the Face of High-Tech with Black Girls Code." *Vanderbilt Magazine*, September 26, 2014. https://news.vanderbilt.edu/ vanderbiltmagazine/kimberly-bryant-is-changing-the-face-of-high-tech-with-black-girls-code.

Gilpin, Lyndsey. "Black Girls Code Founder Kimberly Bryant: Engineer. Entrepreneur. Mother." TechRepublic, April 7, 2014. http://www.techrepublic.com/article/black-girls-code-founder-kimberly-bryant-engineer-entrepreneur-mother.

Greenlee, Greg. "#BITTechTalk with Guest Kimberly Bryant." Blacks in Technology podcast, Episode 23, November 17, 2011. https://www.blacksintechnology.net/bittechtalk-episode-23-with-guest-kimberly-bryant.

Hanselman, Scott. "Improving Diversity in Technology with Kimberly Bryant from BlackGirlsCode.com." Hanselminutes podcast, Show 303, January 26, 2012. http://hanselminutes. com/303/improving-diversity-in-technology-with-kimberly-bryant-from-blackgirlscodecom.

Hill, Catherine, Christianne Corbett, and Andresse St. Rose. "Why So Few? Women in Science, Technology, Engineering, and Mathematics." Washington, DC: AAUW, 2010. https:// www.aauw.org/files/2013/02/Why-So-Few-Women-in-Science-Technology-Engineering-and-Mathematics.pdf.

Kennedy, John. "Kimberly Bryant: 'We Want to Introduce 1m Girls to Coding by 2040' (Video)." *Silicon Republic*, June 19,

2015. https://www.siliconrepublic.com/people/we-want-to-introduce-1m-girls-to-coding-by-2040-kimberly-bryant-tells-inspirefest.

Khan, Sal. "Sal Khan with Black Girls Code's Kimberly Bryant." INFORUM at the Commonwealth Club, YouTube video, April 8, 2015. https://www.youtube.com/watch?v=Yeb8TuuTdwg.

OneDublin.org. "Black Girls Code Founder Kimberly Bryant on Inspiring Students to Pursue STEM." OneDublin.org, January 20, 2014. https://onedublin.org/2014/01/20/black-girls-code-founder-kimberly-bryant-on-inspiring-students-to-pursue-stem.

Pratt, Mary K. "Black Girls Code Founder Looks to Expand Skills Outreach, Challenges CIOs to Help the Cause." *Computer World*, February 11, 2015. http://www.computerworld.com/article/2877211/black-girls-code-founder-looks-to-expand-skills-outreach-challenges-cios-to-help-the-cause.html.

Rosenberg, Debra. "Could This Be the Answer to the Tech World's Diversity Problem?" *Smithsonian*, November 2014. http://www.smithsonianmag.com/innovation/answer-tech-worlds-diversity-problem-180953046/#qCpDq1gLZ8ARbeYt.99.

Smith, Megan. "Computer Science For All." White House, January 30, 2016. https://www.whitehouse.gov/blog/2016/01/30/computer-science-all.

Spiegel, Amy Rose. "Black Girls Code Founder Kimberly Bryant Talks Her Favorite Apps, Diversity in the Tech World, and More." *Complex*, October 24, 2016. http://www.complex.com/life/2016/10/black-girls-code-kimberly-bryant-interview.

Tafoya, Angela. "This Woman Could Change Everything You Believe About Tech: Superwoman Kimberly Bryant."

Refinery29, September 8, 2014. http://www.refinery29.com/ kimberly-bryant.

Vanity Fair Studios with IBM. "Saluting a New Guard of STEM Stars, Part 2." *Vanity Fair*, December 2016. http://www. vanityfair.com/news/2016/12/saluting-a-new-guard-of-stem-stars-part-2.

Wan, Tony. "Where Diversity, Inclusion and Education Meet: A Conversation with Black Girls Code Founder, Kimberly Bryant." EdSurge News, October 23, 2016. https://www. edsurge.com/news/2016-10-23-where-diversity-inclusion-and-education-meet-a-conversation-with-black-girls-code-founder-kimberly-bryant.

INDEX

ABOUT THE AUTHOR

Kathryn Hulick is a freelance writer, editor, and former Peace Corps volunteer. She has written numerous nonfiction books for children, including *Pop Culture: American Life and Video Games*, *Awesome Science: Dinosaurs*, *Artificial Intelligence*, and *Energy Technology*. She also contributes regularly to *Muse* magazine and the Science News for Students website. She enjoys hiking, gardening, painting, and reading. She lives in Massachusetts with her husband, son, and dog. Learn more about her work at kathrynhulick.com.